Help for the Post-abortion Woman

Teri Reisser, M.S., Paul Reisser, M.D.

PYRANEE
BOOKS

Zondervan Publishing House
Grand Rapids, Michigan

Pyranee Books
are published by
Zondervan Publishing House
1415 Lake Dr., S.E.
Grand Rapids, MI 49506

Library of Congress Cataloging-in-Publication Data

Reisser, Teri K.
  Help for the post-abortion woman / by Teri and Paul Reisser.
    p. cm.
  "Pyranee books."
  Bibliography: p.
  ISBN 0-310-34332-1
  1. Abortion—United States—Psychological aspects. 2. Abortion—
Religious aspects—Christianity. 3. Abortion counseling—United
States. I. Reisser, Paul C. II. Title.
HQ767.5.U5R45 1989
363.4'6'019—dc20   89–34338
                                                            CIP

Unless otherwise noted, Scripture quotations are taken from the *Holy Bible: New International Version* (North American Edition), copyright © 1973, 1978, 1984 by The International Bible Society. Used by permission of Zondervan Bible Publishers.

THE CASE HISTORIES IN THIS BOOK ARE TRUE. THE NAMES HAVE BEEN CHANGED EXCEPT FOR REFERENCES TO THE AUTHOR. THE "I" IN THIS BOOK REFERS TO TERI.

Edited by Nia Jones and Judy Hardy

Printed in the United States of America

89 90 91 92 93 94 95 / LP / 10 9 8 7 6 5 4 3 2 1

Contents

Preface

In 1985 we took an active part in the formation of a crisis pregnancy center (CPC) in our community. Like hundreds of other CPCs in the United States, our local center is a labor of love dedicated to supporting alternatives to abortion for women whose pregnancies are a major problem in their lives. As director of the center, Teri was approached, before and during the early months of its operation, by several women who wanted to talk about past abortions, not current pregnancies. Their comments were quite surprising.

All of these women appeared to be functioning well in their everyday lives. Yet in telling their stories (usually about abortions which had occurred years before) they would express intense emotion, often stopping for several minutes of quiet weeping. Most of them stated that they had never described their experiences to anyone, and a few even realized that they had completely suppressed the memory of another abortion.

None of these women had been solicited to tell their story, nor had they recently been whipped into a frenzy at an emotional pro-life rally. Furthermore, none of them told horror stories about back-alley procedures. Most of the abortions had been perfectly legal, and were carried out by competent physicians. The women were simply carrying a very deep pain, which had been walled off like a dormant infection, but which also at times influenced other areas of their lives.

Teri was fascinated and deeply moved by these encounters. Equally fascinating, a computer search of thousands of articles in psychology written over the past several years yielded only fourteen references on the subject of emotional problems following abortion.[1] These articles, and many of the books on abortion written for the general public, offered the same conclusion: any kind of significant emotional reaction following abortion was extremely rare. Some women might have a short case of "the blues" afterwards, but this could be explained by changes in hormone levels after the pregnancy ended.

Over the next several months, hundreds of encounters with women who were experiencing pain in the wake of abortion convinced Teri that psychological and spiritual suffering following abortion is not at all uncommon, and hormonal changes or "the blues" are woefully inadequate explanations for a disturbance which may continue for many years. A number of researchers and therapists nationwide have observed similar patterns, leading to the coining of the term "Post Abortion Syndrome" (PAS).

Many conferences and workshops have subsequently served to clarify the dimensions of Post Abortion Syndrome, and have led to the development of approaches to recovery. In recent months, Teri has conducted a number of seminars on PAS, some under the auspices of the Post Abortion Counseling and Education (or PACE) program of the Christian Action Council. This book contains much of

[1] Since 1985, many more articles have been written on the emotional aftermath of abortion.

the seminar material and is written for two audiences: first, for women who are (or think they may be) suffering in the wake of abortion; and second, for those who desire, as counselors or loving friends, to understand and help women with Post Abortion Syndrome.

One brief note on terminology: throughout this book we frequently use the terms "pro-life" and "pro-choice" to refer to the opposing forces in the ongoing abortion controversy. Although each term encompasses a spectrum of opinions, we will assume that "pro-life" refers to the position that the fetus is a human being entitled to legal protection and that abortion is therefore inherently wrong, and that "pro-choice" designates the viewpoint that a pregnant woman has the ultimate right to decide, on whatever basis, whether or not to continue her pregnancy.

We want to express our loving thanks to Chad and Carrie, who displayed maturity beyond their years while mom and dad worked on this important project.

We are also indebted to the following counselors whose work is reflected in these pages: Linda Ross, Linda Cochrane, Cathy Pisanic, Vincent Rue, Sr. Paula Vandegaer, and Anne Speckhard.

And most importantly, the greatest gratitude goes to the women who experienced healing in the post-abortion groups. Their recovery processes were the building blocks of this book. It is our prayer that their stories will touch the reader and give her hope.

One Woman's Story

• • •

*L*inda's seventeenth birthday was a typical school day. Like the previous 365 days of her life, it came and went without incident. Classes (which had rudely brought summer to a halt only a week before) proceeded in an orderly sequence. Lunch offered the usual uninspired fare, hot gossip was in short supply, and nothing resembling romance was on the horizon.

No big deal, they said, but it meant a lot to her. As she watched them rustle through cluttered purses in search of loose change, and listened to their noisy efforts to figure out who had the hots for whom, Linda was struck by how much she was like them: neither rich nor broke, neither brilliant nor dumb, neither gorgeous nor ugly. Similar homes, similar neighborhoods, similar families—indeed, their common ground included the fact that nearly everyone's parents, including hers, had been divorced.

For Linda, this event had come at the worst possible time, during an eighth-grade semester which felt like four months of fingernails on the chalkboard. The muffled sounds of her mom and dad fighting late at night turned Linda's stomach inside out, and their separation didn't provide much relief. Her dad settled into a condo and a new relationship not long after the ink had dried on the legal papers, and Linda spent every other weekend with him in a futile effort to stay close. By her seventeenth birthday, her visits came only every other month. Linda's mom tried to keep the house and her wounds in reasonable condition, and the two of them managed to have some good times together as Linda emerged from the uncivilized world of junior high school. But eventually Linda started dating.

Perhaps Linda's mom was still smarting from her husband's sudden departure for greener (and younger) pastures. Maybe she had spent too many years worrying about her little girl's entry into womanhood. Or could it be that she had a few high-school secrets of her own? Whatever the cause, Linda was dismayed by her mom's scrutiny of every member of the opposite sex who came within a block of the front door. Even the simplest date seemed to produce a congressional investigation the next morning. And the going got tougher after Linda met Steven. He was polite, intelligent, and above all attentive to Linda in ways no one had been before. Within a few weeks the shallow rituals of dating gave way to long talks, deep emotion, and the inevitable desire for intimacy. As her dream of married life with Steven after graduation became more focused, Linda's old list of dos and don'ts slowly faded from memory. Their relationship intensified, and so did her mother's continual lectures about getting "too serious" with him. But Linda held her ground.

On the first day of spring break, Linda drove several miles to a drugstore in another community, made a purchase, and then slipped into the ladies' room of a nearby coffee shop. She read and reread the directions on the test she had bought, then watched with horror as it quietly informed her that she was pregnant. How could this have happened when they had been so careful?

She called Steven, who drove over immediately and met her with support, reassurance, and a very specific resolve. He was surprisingly calm, as if he had expected this conversation and had rehearsed his lines. While she stared at her soft drink and fiddled with the pregnancy test, he spelled out his conclusion that an abortion would be the only sensible solution to their problem. He would even pay for it. But somewhere in the distant past Linda had concluded that abortion was wrong. Now, for the first time, she said so. Thus began their very first serious fight.

Unfortunately, the alternatives to abortion appeared dismal, and Steven wasted no time painting several gloomy pictures. How would her mom react after all the big lectures about "going too far"? She would probably try to ground Linda for the next decade, and life without Steven would be unbearable. What about her dad? He was so wrapped up with his new wife and her two kids that he wanted little more than an occasional phone call from Linda informing him that his own little girl was "just fine." A problem like this would kill him, if he didn't kill her (or Steven) first. And how about college? Who wants to have a baby in the middle of her freshman year? Who would pay the bills? The idea of changing diapers in the middle of a cram session for midterms sounded ridiculous.

The argument ended in a lopsided stalemate: Linda held her ground about the abortion. She realized, though, that Steven was probably right. She was being too emotional about this decision, and not thinking logically. Still, when they parted that afternoon, their embrace lacked its usual intensity.

The powerful feeling of comfort and abandon Linda usually felt in Steven's arms had changed. It would never be the same again.

Only two of Linda's most trusted friends heard about the pregnancy and the fight, and both said without a moment's hesitation that even considering having the baby was crazy. All of her hopes and plans with Steven would have to be seriously revised. And, they predicted, Steven would probably start looking elsewhere once Linda's bikini refused to fit. Before spring break ended, Linda had agreed to let Steven schedule the abortion.

On the appointed day, Linda and Steven drove across town to a women's health center. The receptionist was friendly, brisk, and efficient, and a counselor assured her that the procedure was no worse than having a wisdom tooth extracted. When she began to express some doubts, she was reminded that only she could make the decision, but that her doubts weren't all that unusual. Did she want to go home and think it over? Linda quickly replayed the argument with Steven and the gloomy scenarios of a pregnancy turning her life upside down. She sighed, then decided to get this over with. The counselor affirmed her decision and assured her she would be just fine.

When she returned to the waiting room, Linda was amazed by the low-key atmosphere. Some women were chatting with one another as though they were waiting for a bus, while others leafed through fashion magazines. No one entering or leaving the clinic seemed to be upset. The counselor was probably right—she would be just fine.

Linda retained control through the bored greeting by a doctor who forgot to introduce himself, the sting of the anesthetic, the cramping, the suction noises, the sound of something going through a plastic tube. But when it was all over, she wept inconsolably, as if grieving a terrible loss. The nurse wasn't much help as Linda sobbed quietly in the recovery area. There just wasn't enough time to hold anyone's hand on a busy morning like this.

On the drive home, Steven couldn't think of much to say. He was very attentive for a few days but eventually became irritated by her mood swings. Gradually a coolness crept into their relationship, and when Steven finally suggested that they break up, Linda felt surprisingly indifferent. By the time graduation day arrived, she had stopped thinking about Steven, wedding plans, or the abortion.

Linda spent the next four years immersed in college life. She studied hard and dated a lot, being careful not to develop emotional ties to anyone in particular, and never forgetting to take her birth control pills. Like a scar, the combination of a busy schedule and a sense of numbness protected her from feeling anything too deeply. But two years after graduation she met John, who seemed to ride into her life like Prince Charming. Before long he resurrected feelings she had avoided for years. A flurry of dates led to an engagement ring presented with great finesse during a candlelight dinner, and a wedding six months later.

As their first anniversary drew near, John began talking about starting a family. Not much had been said about this over the preceding months, and now for some reason John's most casual comments about little people running around the house set off a quiet panic inside Linda. She avoided the subject as much as possible, but eventually a few romantic evenings and John's smoothest talk over wine and fresh flowers proved irresistible. What could be better than to raise children with such a wonderful husband?

Yet as they officially trashed her birth-control pills in an impromptu ceremony, a growing depression began to crowd in on Linda like a gathering storm. She manufactured reasons to avoid sex, especially midway through her cycle. She found herself awakening, cold and covered with sweat, in the middle of the night, trying to remember the details of nightmares having to do with babies or lost children.

When John's sister and her husband arrived for a weekend to show off their newborn daughter, Linda could barely make conversation. After this awkward visit ended, she began thinking about the baby she had aborted. With her thoughts came an uncontrolled flood of tears at odd hours of the day. Even a Pampers commercial would provoke a hasty departure to the bathroom in search of Kleenex.

Increasingly concerned about his wife's moods, John managed one night to convince Linda to talk about what was bothering her. She had kept her abortion a secret from him until now, and he did an admirable job of listening to her story. But afterwards his nightly jogging session became a feverish sprint as wretched images tore through his mind again and again. He knew Linda had not been inexperienced when they met (nor had he), but somehow her abortion, though now only a memory, had become an ugly and powerful intruder in their marriage. There was no way they could work past this pain without some help.

During Linda's first session with the marriage counselor she was encouraged to ventilate her feelings toward those involved in the abortion experience. A venomous blast against her parents and Steven surprised Linda and impressed the therapist. The experience was cathartic, and she went home feeling better than she had in months. But in three days she had plummeted to a new level of depression.

When Linda brought up the abortion again the following week, the counselor assured her that a past abortion could not be the cause of a serious depression and that they needed to leave the abortion behind in order to focus on her present relationships. They had other work to do, and she could not continue dwelling on this single episode as an excuse for her present condition. In addition, the counselor recommended that she might be a candidate for anti-depressant medication and arranged for a brief psychiatric consultation to explore this option.

After another month of tears, fitful sleep and a dry mouth from her new medication, Linda felt confused and discouraged. As she lay next to John on a muggy Thursday night, all she could think about was what a colossal mess she had made of her life. *Why bother with the endless, expensive therapy sessions? John is spending so much on a problem he had nothing to do with—maybe he'd be better off without me. And who needs this drug and all its lousy side effects?*

I think I'll flush them down the toilet. On second thought, maybe I should just take them all at once . . .

• • •

Should I Read This Book?

L inda's story in the previous chapter is a composite of several women's experiences. Although the names and some other identifying elements have been changed (as they have been in other stories throughout this book), the events are true. They are also by no means unique.

This year thousands of "Lindas" will become pregnant when they least want or expect to be. They will agonize over their pregnancy and their circumstances—perhaps by themselves, but more often with the baby's father, or their girlfriends, or perhaps their parents. They will decide to have an abortion, but with very mixed feelings. They will feel some relief at first, but months (or more often years) later will begin experiencing emotional pain which may become disabling. And they may consult a counselor or therapist who does not recognize, or will trivialize, the role one or more past abortions is playing in their current emotional turmoil.

Perhaps, in one or more ways, you are like Linda. You may be convinced that (or wondering if) your depression, or anxiety, or nightmares, or any of a dozen other symptoms are related to an abortion in your past. You may have scanned the titles of multitudes of self-help books in your local bookstore, looking for one which would at least confirm that an abortion might continue to cause problems, even years after the procedure.

Perhaps you have never told your "secret" to anyone

else, because you fear their reaction. Yet with one out of four pregnancies ending in abortion in America for the past several years, it is likely that one or more women you know share the same secret. Many women who appear calm and competent on the surface may be struggling with the same issues, but are afraid to bring them up. After all, even women who firmly believe in the right to have an abortion rarely relish talking about their own. This is not a likely topic for the dinner table, or conversation over the back fence, or the Wednesday night prayer meeting, or even a close support group.

If you have had an abortion within the past several weeks and have been in acute emotional pain ever since, your inability to deny the conflict you feel may work in your favor—if you address that pain NOW. By doing so, you will save yourself years of disruption caused by driving that pain into your subconscious. Unfortunately, the majority of women who have experienced distress shortly after an abortion endure years of unhealthy relationships and living patterns before finally coming to the point where they deal with the pain.

If you are many years from your abortion experience, you may feel as if you have two competing voices inside you—one that keeps insisting that you are doing just fine with the abortion, and another that reminds you that your conflict has never been settled. If you have recently started thinking about it again, it is probably time to give the second voice a chance to be heard. Listening to it may seem a terrifying proposition, but the longer you refuse to listen the harder it will be to face and deal with the painful memories you cannot forever keep repressed.

Below are some key questions to ask yourself.[1] Be

[1] Most of these questions are taken from the excellent post-abortion workbook, *Women in Ramah*, authored by a dear friend and gifted

honest and pay attention to any emotional or physical reactions you may have to particular questions. These will give you some important clues as to whether you need healing from a previous abortion:

1. Do you find yourself struggling to turn off feelings connected to your abortion(s), perhaps telling yourself over and over again to forget about it?
2. Do you find yourself avoiding books, magazines and television programs that deal with the subject of abortion?
3. Are you affected by physical reminders of your abortion (babies, pregnant women, etc.)? Are you uncomfortable around children?
4. Are there certain times of the year you find yourself depressed, sick or accident-prone— especially around the anniversary date of the abortion or the would-be birth date?
5. Are you resentful and unforgiving toward any-one because of his or her involvement in your abortion(s)—parents, boyfriend, abortionist, friends, or husband?
6. Are you in a situation where you could find yourself faced with another unwanted preg-nancy?
7. Do you have trouble with emotional intimacy since your abortion?
8. Have you experienced periods of prolonged depression since your abortion? Have you had any suicidal thoughts?
9. Have you experienced any peculiar occurrences

woman, Linda Cochrane, and published by the Christian Action Council.

relating to the abortion experience, such as nightmares about babies, flashbacks, or hallucinations (for example, hearing a baby cry)?

10. Are you able to talk about abortion? When choosing to share about your abortion(s), are you overcome with strong feelings?

11. If you have children now, do you smother them with your love or overprotect them? Are you unable to bond with the children you now have?

12. If you do not have children, do you fear that you will never be able to have them (either because of physical harm resulting from the abortion or because God won't allow you)?

13. Do you tend to look at your life in terms of "before" and "after" the abortion(s)? Has your self-concept changed?

14. Have you found yourself preoccupied with thoughts of your aborted child lately?

15. Did your relationship to or concept of God change after your abortion? How?

If you answered one or more of the above questions "yes," and especially if you had an emotional or physical response to any of them, you are probably suffering from a problem known as Post Abortion Syndrome. You will most likely benefit from exploring the contents of this book.

We hope that the information offered in the following chapters will help you understand what happened to you emotionally during and after the time of your abortion and, more importantly, help you experience healing for the guilt, anger, and/or grief you may feel. (See bibliography for ordering information.)

The Silent Epidemic

*M*any of us remember the late 1960s and early 1970s as a time of widespread sit-ins and marches protesting America's involvement in the Vietnam war. At the same time, a smaller movement was intensely protesting America's abortion laws. Before the Supreme Court wrote its landmark *Roe v. Wade* decision of 1973, most states either restricted or completely outlawed abortion. Individuals and groups working to legalize abortion (such as the National Association for the Repeal of Abortion Laws—NARAL) argued vigorously that women who had to carry unwanted pregnancies were inevitably victimized in two ways.

First, they claimed that women who were forced to deliver babies they didn't want often suffered great emotional distress. In fact, prior to 1973 a number of states allowed a woman to abort if a psychiatrist would declare that severe psychological harm would occur if the pregnancy continued. In some cities, pro-abortion therapists were more than willing to escort women quickly through this requirement, without a detailed evaluation. This argument made a very important assumption: if denying an abortion to a woman who desperately wanted one would harm her psychologically, then allowing her to have one would make her psychologically well.

The other pre-1973 argument for legalizing abortion is still raised automatically today whenever any restriction on abortion is proposed. Women who were desperate to end their pregnancies would subject themselves to "back-alley" abortionists. Those who survived the incompetent medical care often told horror stories of searing pain, humiliation, and overt sexual harassment by their "doctor." There was (and is) no question that these experiences scarred thousands of women, physically and emotionally. In contrast to such disasters, the idea of a legal abortion carried out by a well-trained physician, in a clinic staffed by supportive counselors and nurses, seemed like a heavenly vision.

Thus, when abortion suddenly became readily available in 1973, few people stopped to ponder whether legal and relatively safe abortions might cause significant problems. Since that time, a vocal contingent of speakers, authors, and professionals has continued to insist that abortion has no important emotional consequences, unless a woman is already unbalanced. Consider the following examples:

In a 1988 radio discussion, the director of Planned Parenthood in Los Angeles stated flatly that only a hundred or so women every year (out of 1.5 million who have abortions nationwide) experience any subsequent, significant emotional distress. It is unlikely, of course, that a major abortion provider would be inclined to sound a warning about its own service, but this figure represents an astonishing confidence on Planned Parenthood's part that so little could go wrong. In just three years, drawing from our own community with a population of 100,000, Teri has worked in depth with well over a hundred women who have experienced major emotional problems in the wake of an abortion. (These women sought counseling on their own initiative, based on a yellow pages ad for the Crisis Pregnancy Center which included "Post-abortion Counseling.")

Many books written for the general public are more

blunt in their conviction that having an abortion shouldn't give anyone much grief. A popular collection of health information for women is *The New Our Bodies, Ourselves*, a 1984 revision of the best-selling *Our Bodies, Ourselves*. In a section entitled "Feelings After an Abortion," the authors state,

> Severe depression after an abortion is extremely rare. In fact, it is much less likely than severe depression after childbirth. A few women experience feelings of sadness or depression years later at around the time of year when they had the abortion or when they would have given birth.

> Women sometimes feel guilty, which is understandable in a society that doesn't particularly accept the choice of abortion. So much emphasis is put on motherhood that many people act as though a fetus is more important than a woman.

> If you were not able to work through your feelings before the abortion, you may feel troubled afterwards. Being able to talk about your feelings with a sympathetic and objective friend, relative, counselor or group is the most important thing you can do to help you feel better, resolve difficulties and move on.[1]

A relatively new book, *The Abortion Controversy*, discusses abortion procedures, the *Roe v. Wade* decision and its aftermath, and the two sides of the issue in rather plain language geared for a teenage audience. In a section entitled "The Psychological Effects," author Carol Emmons states somewhat blandly,

---

[1] The Boston Women's Health Collective, Ed., *The New Our Bodies, Ourselves* (New York: Simon and Schuster, 1984), p. 307.

An abortion can sometimes cause emotional or psychological problems. They are generally considered minor upsets, however. According to the Institute of Medicine of the National Academy of Sciences, there is no evidence of serious mental illness caused by having an abortion.[2]

She continues by mentioning briefly some reasons why guilt may occur after abortion, but then concludes with the statement:

It is worth noting that more women are depressed following childbirth than following an abortion. After childbirth, many women have the "baby blues," or postpartum depression. In part, this feeling is caused by hormonal changes in the body.[3]

The role of hormones in post-abortion emotions is a common theme in other books written for lay audiences.[4] This explanation, of course, offers little insight into any prolonged or delayed feelings of guilt or despair which a woman might experience. Authors Maria Corsaro and

[2]Carol A. Emmons, *The Abortion Controversy* (New York: Julian Messner, 1987), p. 18.

[3]Ibid., p. 21.

[4]Beryl Lieff Benderly, in her book *Thinking About Abortion* (Garden City, New York: The Dial Press, 1984, p.131) writes:

But what about the emotions, which have played such a vital part in the woman's experience? This answer often involves . . . the hormones. . . . Although many women feel relief as their overriding, immediate and lasting reaction, many also report "the blues," "the dumps," or a "funk" for the next few days. This usually isn't a serious depression but rather the same "down" feeling that plagues many women every month with their periods or right after they deliver a baby. And it comes from the same cause: hormone swings often mean mood swings as well.

Carole Korzeniowsky, in *A Woman's Guide to Safe Abortion*, elaborate on the hormonal situation and offer a few additional reasons why one might feel unhappy after an abortion:

> Many women feel slightly "down" after the abortion. This may be connected with the hormonal change. If you've felt this sort of thing before, during your monthly ovulation or menstruation, then you know what we mean. Added to that, of course, is the strain of rushing around to arrange for tests and the abortion, and the physical stress of the operation itself. So if you feel a little weepy and shaky, it's very understandable. . . .

> If you're having any of these feelings after the abortion, it can help to know that many women feel the same way. A few tears and a tinge of the blues is perfectly normal in the first few days.[5]

A similar viewpoint prevails in the books and journal articles written by and for physicians and psychologists. For example, the current edition of a standard, widely distributed psychiatry textbook devotes a major portion of its section on abortion to the stress of carrying an unwanted pregnancy.[6] This would seem to be an odd subject to cover at a time when abortion is so readily available, but it reveals a notion expressed in much of the professional literature: the problems caused by abortions

[5] Maria Corsaro and Carole Korzeniowsky, *A Woman's Guide to Safe Abortion* (New York: Holt, Rinehart and Winston, 1983), pp. 47, 58.

[6] Judith E. Belsky, M.D., Livia S. Wan, M.D., and Gordon W. Douglas, M.D., "Abortion," in Harold I. Kaplan, M.D. and Benjamin J. Sadock, M.D., Eds., *Comprehensive Textbook of Psychiatry* (Baltimore: Williams and Witkins, 1985), pp. 1052–56.

re trivial compared to those brought by having a child under stressful (or even ideal) circumstances.[7]

More recently, in January 1989, the American Psychological Association (APA) stated that its survey of the current professional literature indicated that most women do not suffer lasting effects from abortion. Brian Wilcox, Director of Public Interest Legislation for the APA, stated, "It's clear that the vast majority of women are not going to experience any significant problems. Millions of women are having abortions, and it appears to be a relatively benign procedure both medically and psychologically."[8] Yet as impressive as this statement and others like it sound, they simply do not tell the whole story. Over the past few years, a serious challenge to the notion that abortion is "a relatively benign procedure" has arisen.

In 1982, Nancyjo Mann established a group called Women Exploited by Abortion (WEBA). Her goal was to offer support and a voice for women who, like herself, felt they had been damaged by a past abortion. As Ms. Mann appeared on radio and television interviews, thousands of women discovered that they were not alone in their pain. Many literally came out of the closet in order to join WEBA support groups, which today are meeting in every state of the country.

In scattered locations throughout the United States, a

[7]Similarly, medical textbooks which list the possible physical complications of abortion inevitably add a comment that, statistically, abortion is safer than normal childbirth. This is, of course, useless information, not unlike saying that it is statistically safer to stay in the house than to go outside. Staying indoors may be safer, but very few of us take this into consideration when we need groceries. Likewise, even if abortion is statistically safer than childbirth, only a fool would propose that all pregnancies be terminated.

[8]"Study: Abortion Harm Doesn't Last," News Chronicle, 25 (January 1989), sec. 1, p. 11.

few therapists began listening to women who we
reporting pain after their abortions, and taking the
seriously. As they located one another and compare
notes, they noticed striking similarities in their pos
abortion clients. There appeared to be much more to th
issue than a few unbalanced women whining about the
abortions. There were instead thousands, perhaps m
lions, of women for whom abortion had not spelle
"relief," but rather heartache and even despair.

Pioneer researchers such as Drs. Anne Speckhar
Vincent Rue, and David Reardon began organizing an
publishing their findings, eventually coining the ter
"Post Abortion Syndrome" (or PAS) to describe th
condition they saw repeatedly. Most investigators in th
new field came to agree with Anne Speckhard's definitio
of PAS: a woman's chronic inability to: (1) process th
fear, anger, sadness and guilt surrounding her abortio
experience, (2) grieve (or even name) the loss of her bab
and (3) come to peace with God, herself, and othe
involved in the abortion decision. (Most therapists in th
field acknowledge that any person involved in the abo
tion decision is also a possible candidate for PAS.)

They also took a hard look at the journal article
which had concluded that few women were trouble
following abortion and found some serious weaknesses i
the way these studies were performed and written
Meanwhile, books detailing individual post-abortion exp
riences of pain and subsequent healing began to appea
on the market for the general public. (*Will I Cry Tomorrow*
by Susan Stanford, *Helping Women Recover from Abortion* b

[9]The details of their work are too involved to review in this book. I
essence, they have found weaknesses in the methods of collectir
information from women following their abortion, as well as examples
bias in the interpretation of data.

Nancy Michels, *Beyond Choice* by Don Baker and *Abortion's Second Victim* by Pam Koerbel are examples.)

Concern with the effects of abortion on women eventually reached the highest levels of government. In 1987 President Reagan ordered Surgeon General C. Everett Koop to review the medical and psychological risks of abortion and report his findings to the public. In January 1989, Dr. Koop reported only that he could not draw sweeping conclusions from the scientific evidence currently available. Instead he urged that a large-scale, comprehensive study be organized, one that could take five years to complete and potentially cost 100 million dollars.

The bottom line is this: Far too many women (and men) are suffering emotional pain resulting from an abortion to be ignored, even though scientific research has not fully defined the scope of the problem. No one knows how many women are affected, but there are good reasons to believe that the number extends into the hundreds of thousands.

Deep and usually conflicting emotions are a part of nearly every abortion decision. To consider an abortion to be a trivial event in a woman's life (equivalent to having a wisdom tooth extracted, as too many abortion clinics suggest) is naive indeed. A sizable number of women enter clinics and hospitals believing that abortion is wrong, but convinced that they have no other reasonable choice. One 1981 opinion poll of 1,105 women, compiled in part by a sociologist from Planned Parenthood's own research organization, found that 24 percent of women who had had abortions considered the procedure morally wrong.[10] Assuming that this percentage is still accurate, at

[10] The study was conducted by Greg Martire of the opinion research corporation Yankelovich, Skelly and White, and by Stanley K. Henshaw

least one out of four women having an abortion (ov*
350,000 every year) is violating her own moral standard
(This, in fact, is one of the most common issues reporte*
by women who seek help months or years after a
abortion.)

Overall, the problem involves more than statistics an*
journal articles. There are thousands of individuals wh*
have been deeply affected by abortion and who nee*
healing. As Post Abortion Syndrome has been mor*
widely discussed and debated in the media, more wome*
(as well as men, siblings, and parents) are coming forwar*
to find the help they so badly need. In the course of he*
lecturing across the country on the subject of PAS, Te*
has had conversations with hundreds of post-abortio*
women who were willing to travel long distances to see*
help, and who have been bewildered by the ignorance o*
local therapists on this issue.

For those who are now realizing that they need help*
or who know someone who does, it is important t*
understand the symptoms which can occur sooner or late*
after an abortion—what they are, and how they start*

of the Alan Guttmacher Institute, the research arm of Planned Parent*
hood. Reported in "Abortion Clinics' Toughest Cases," *Medical Worl*
News* (March 9, 1987), 56.

How Does Post Abortion Syndrome Develop?

I n late 1986, American movie audiences experienced the Vietnam war through the vivid images of a powerful film. "Platoon" graphically portrayed the terror of combat from the foot-soldier's viewpoint. It also tied enough stomachs in knots to win the Academy Award for Best Picture of the Year. Unfortunately, a number of viewers who had actually been in the war experienced more than a loss of appetite: they actually suffered emotional breakdowns during or after the show. Why would this happen to people who had simply watched a film? The answer is important both to combat veterans and to many women who have experienced an abortion.

For more than a decade beginning in the late 1960s, psychologists working with soldiers who had served in Vietnam observed an alarming pattern. Men who previously had been well-adjusted were literally haunted by their experiences overseas. They could not rid themselves of recurring thoughts, images and dreams of the war. Many suffered disturbing symptoms such as sweating, pounding of the heart, and outbursts of anger or fear. Difficulty with relationships and abuse of alcohol or drugs (an escape used by many during their tour of duty) were not unusual. In a typical situation, a young veteran might panic and dive for cover during a small-town fireworks show. And, more recently, former soldiers who walked into a showing of "Platoon" experienced a massive and disabling flashback, even though the war had been ove[r] for twelve years.

Therapists who worked with these men eventuall[y] described a syndrome which they called "Post Traumati[c] Stress Disorder" (PTSD). Because the Vietnam war ha[d] been such a politically and emotionally explosive issue i[n] this country, pioneer researchers found it difficult t[o] convince many of their colleagues that this disorder trul[y] existed, and that many returning veterans were it[s] victims. (Indeed, twelve years elapsed before PTSD finall[y] received formal recognition as a psychiatric diagnosis.[)]

Psychologists have since found that PTSD can affec[t] anyone who has suffered through an intense and trau[-] matic event which is not a part of normal experience—fo[r] example, close combat, a natural disaster (earthquake[,] flood, etc.), a serious accident, or a violent incident suc[h] as torture or rape. All too often, victims of such episode[s] do not simply pick up with their lives where they left off[.] Instead, they undergo a variety of reactions which do no[t] fade away with the passage of time. Many symptoms ma[y] not even become evident until years have passed. Thes[e] typically include obsessive and intense memories of th[e] event, a driving need to avoid anything which might brin[g] it to mind, and a list of associated symptoms (includin[g] sleeping problems, eating and sexual disorders, depres[-] sion, and so forth).

A number of therapists who have interviewed an[d] counseled women who have had an abortion have notice[d] similar or identical patterns of reaction to those we jus[t] listed. It appears, in fact, that Post Abortion Syndrome is [a] specific form of Post Traumatic Stress Disorder. Many o[f] the details vary from case to case, and not all wome[n] experience a disturbing reaction in the months or year[s] after an abortion. But for those who do (and we believe[d]) the number to be significant), there are some specific factors involved and a common pattern of symptoms.

How Does Post Abortion Syndrome Develop?

For any form of Post Traumatic Stress Disorder to occur, there must be an event which is both traumatic and beyond the normal range of human experience. In the case of a war or disaster, the terror of the event is obvious. But abortion in the United States is legal and socially sanctioned, and over 4,000 procedures occur every day. Why would having an abortion be traumatic?

First of all, most women approach an abortion decision in a state of crisis. Discovering that one is pregnant is an emotionally charged moment, normally the cause either for great rejoicing or for terrible alarm. If the pregnancy represents a major problem, a woman will experience a tremendous amount of fear and anxiety, which will drive her either to seek a fast solution or to avoid dealing with it as long as possible.

Eventually she must make some sort of decision. But unlike most other decisions in life, the abortion decision is likely to be affected by deeply rooted moral convictions, by strong opinions from family/boyfriend/husband, by mixed feelings about intimacy and sexuality, and by physical changes in her body. It may be discussed with a counselor or a close friend, but it won't be the subject of casual conversation. Thus, even though abortion is legal and to some degree socially sanctioned, and even though she may know someone who has had one, deciding to end a pregnancy still falls well outside the realm of most women's normal experience. It will remain the woman's very uncomfortable secret, not her badge of honor.

Aside from the intensity of the decision to have an

abortion, several other factors may predispose a woman to emotional turmoil in the near or distant future:

1. First and foremost, it is not at all uncommon for a woman to have mixed feelings (for any number of reasons) about the decision to abort. The more difficult the decision, the more likely that the positive feelings about having the baby will resurface later, when the reasons for the abortion seem less compelling.

• • •

After three weeks of wavering between a desire to carry and a resolve to abort, Margaret finally agreed with her fiancé that a baby would completely disrupt their career plans. Once the procedure was over, she firmly put the episode behind her and plunged into finishing her MBA degree. The engagement didn't work out, but Margaret was successful in climbing the corporate ladder.

Twelve years later, Margaret found herself thinking about once-cherished dreams of marriage and children. Within one year she was married and vigorously threw herself into the happy task of getting pregnant—but she could not. As the months passed, Margaret found herself beginning to think more and more often of the baby so easily conceived years ago. The thoughts turned to yearning, and the yearning to a full-blown depression. And Margaret began, for the first time, wondering whether there was a corporate ladder high enough to climb away from the pain of going through life childless.

• • •

2. A woman having an abortion may be directly violating her own moral code. Whether she has a mild uneasiness about abortion, or is violently opposed to it, any woman may reach a point where she feels that her own circumstances leave her no other option. Nearly every abortion clinic director has some "war stories" about women who were picketing the facility one week and entering as a client the next.[1]

Immediately after the procedure, such a woman will usually feel profound relief that the crisis is over, for better or worse. But any moral struggle she felt prior to the abortion will eventually surface again, at which point she will question her decision. The more intense the struggle, the more unpleasant the subsequent feelings are likely to be. In some cases, a woman who originally was comfortable with her abortion decision may undergo a change in moral perspective later in life. This can also lead to great uncertainty about her past choice.

3. A woman who feels that she was forced into the decision by others (parents, boyfriend, husband) is likely to feel anger and bitterness if her abortion becomes an issue later in her life.

• • •

As a child Jean endured her parents' extremely stormy divorce, and as a result became a passive and dependent adult. Though attractive, she generally avoided dating. She was, however, attracted to Alan, who was her opposite: self-assured, a smooth talker,

[1]The problem of the staunch pro-life woman who requests an abortion for herself or her daughter was discussed in a fascinating article in a weekly newsmagazine for physicians. The report encompassed a broad range of women who make an abortion decision in opposition to their own moral standards. ("Abortion Clinics' Toughest Cases," *Medical World News* [March 9, 1987], 55–61.)

used to having his own way. They met each other's needs and were married.

Alan had some very specific plans for their life together. Children were to be spaced far enough apart for his income and their home to accommodate them. As it turned out, Jean had trouble becoming pregnant, such that her first two children seemed to be minor miracles. When her daughters were six and three, she began yearning for a third child, and even offered a tentative prayer to God that she might beat the odds once more. She did.

Alan was upset over the news of a future family member. The timing was wrong. He wanted each child to have an individual bedroom, and moving to a larger house was not on the agenda for this particular year. While his business income was more than adequate to handle expenses, a new baby simply did not fit into his plans. So, after very little discussion, he contacted a privately owned clinic in their community and scheduled Jean's abortion.

Jean did not do well at the clinic. On the morning of her appointment she wept openly as the consent forms were placed in front of her. The clinic staff, noting her obvious turmoil, sent her home to think it over. When Alan came home from work to find Jean still pregnant, he was furious. He made another appointment and personally took her back to the clinic, fuming about the time he had lost from his business to deal with this problem.

Jean's tears were no less obvious as the consent forms came out again, but now Alan stood by to make sure they were signed. He and the doctor both reassured her that "this was the right decision," and the abortion was completed. Months later, Alan could not understand why Jean was so distant, why she cried so much, and why she avoided making love.

• • •

Stories like this seem to be far more common in abortion clinics than in private physicians' offices. Virtually all such facilities are ready and willing to support a woman through an abortion when others are pressuring her to have the baby. Some, however, are amazingly blind to the opposite situation, and will proceed with an abortion when an unhappy woman appears to be submitting to the pressure of others.

4. Limited disclosure of details about the abortion procedure make the initial decision easier. But this can be a time bomb for some very unpleasant emotions later.

A woman signing a consent for abortion usually has only the vaguest notion of what is about to happen. There is virtually never any discussion about the size or state of development of the fetus; rather, the impersonal terms such as "pregnancy tissue" or "products of conception" are used. Since the woman is usually in great turmoil about her decision, she is not likely to ask for too many details. She just wants to get the abortion over with.

• • •

Louise was fifteen weeks into her pregnancy by the time she went to an abortion clinic. Because the pregnancy was so far advanced, the clinic counselor said she would have a procedure called a D & E, which would be "just like the vacuum procedure." The abortion was scheduled for the end of the week. Meanwhile a friend asked Louise to talk with the director of a local crisis pregnancy center offering information and services for alternatives to abortion.

As it turned out, Louise had not actually been told what a D & E is. The initials stand for *d*ilatation and *e*vacuation of the uterus. At this stage of development, the fetus is too large to pass through the vacuum tube normally used in earlier pregnancies. The doctor must therefore use surgical instruments to remove the fetus a piece at a time. (Arms, legs, head, etc., must come separately.)

Louise was astonished to hear this basic explanation, insisting that none of this had been told to her at the clinic. Nevertheless, she still felt that she must have the abortion. The crisis pregnancy center director asked her to do one thing before the day of the appointment: return to the clinic and insist on a full description of the planned procedure, as well as specific information about the size and development of the fetus at 15 weeks.

• • •

One of the most common complaints of women who have come to regret their abortions is that they didn't have all the facts, especially about the fetus growing inside them. At the time a woman may be comforted with a doctor's or counselor's talk about "products of conception," which gives the impression that an abortion does nothing more than remove a shapeless blob of cells. Later she may happen to watch a TV program about the first weeks of life. Perhaps she will see images in a magazine or book. Whatever the source of information, the dawning awareness that what she aborted had arms, legs, and a beating heart can lead to agonizing questions: "Why didn't they tell me it looked like that? If I knew what I know now, I would never have had an abortion."[2]

---

[2]Some have argued that disclosing details about the fetus does little

In 1983 two researchers reported some interesting observations in the prestigious *New England Journal of Medicine*. Two women were scheduled for ultrasound examinations of their early (10 week) pregnancies. One woman had been punched in the abdomen just after becoming pregnant; the other had a possible problem with her hormone balance. Each was asked if she would like to watch the ultrasound screen, and if she would talk about what she saw. Both women had similar reactions to the procedure. The authors described one woman's response:

> She agreed without hesitation, indeed, with a spark of interest in her eyes. One of us pointed to the small, visibly moving fetal form on the screen and asked, "How do you feel about seeing what is inside you?" She answered crisply, "It certainly makes you think twice about abortion!" When asked to say more, she told of the surprise she felt on viewing the fetal form, especially on seeing it move: "I feel that it is human. It belongs to me. I couldn't have an abortion now."[3]

5. Late abortions are more likely to be disturbing sooner or later because the procedures are more compli-

more than make the abortion decision more difficult and increases the risk for emotional suffering later. On the surface this viewpoint sounds valid. But it also flies in the face of the entire concept of informed choice.

A consistent (and valid) goal of the feminist movement has been that of promoting a woman's full participation in medical decisions which affect her. It is ironic that most feminist literature objects to full disclosure about fetal development prior to abortion, preferring instead the old patronizing approach to women from health-care providers. "There, there, dear, don't worry about the details. Doctor knows best.")

[3]John C. Fletcher, Ph.D. and Mark I. Evans, M.D., "Maternal Bonding in Early Fetal Ultrasound Examinations," *New England Journal of Medicine* (February 17, 1983): 392–93.

cated and the outcome looks much more like "killing a baby" than "extracting the contents of the uterus." This is especially true if the pregnancy has progressed far enough to be visible, and if the woman has felt fetal movement before the procedure.

After the fourth month, a pregnancy is ended by injecting a concentrated salt solution into the uterus. The fetus dies (often with vigorous kicking at first), and later the woman goes into labor, delivering what she can easily identify as a small, lifeless baby. The shock of this sight ("I didn't know it was a baby!") may cause her not only regret but a feeling that she was betrayed by her doctor or the abortion clinic. These experiences not only swell the ranks of groups such as Women Exploited by Abortion, but also lead to prolonged anger and bitterness.

6. Issues related to wanted children later in life can rekindle unpleasant aspects of the abortion decision. Most poignant is the situation of a woman who had one or more abortions earlier in life and now is unable to become pregnant when she wants to. The thought of having aborted the only children she ever conceived will be a source of deepest pain and regret.

Similarly, a pregnancy with a wanted child may stir all sorts of memories and mixed emotions about a previous abortion. Focusing attention on the identity and health of the baby to be born raises some pointed issues. This pregnancy involves "my baby," which is to be nurtured and protected; the other consisted of "products of conception" which were destroyed. Realizing that they are biologically identical may be disturbing indeed.

7. A woman who lives in an environment (such as a staunchly religious family) in which her abortion must be kept a deep, dark secret is at greater risk for conflict at some point. While some might argue that her pain in such a case is the product of "repressive" surroundings, it is just as likely that she shares some of the anti-abortion sentiments of those around her.

• • •

One or more of the above situations can make the abortion decision very emotionally charged. Once it is completed, the feeling immediately after an abortion is nearly always relief. For better or worse, a decision was made and the episode appears to be over. (It is this stage of a woman's experience that a number of studies have identified, without following the story further.)

But sooner or later, the issues which upset her previously will be raised again. Since she cannot go back and "undo" the abortion, one of two processes will begin. She may reexperience emotional pain intense enough to drive her to seek help relatively soon after the procedure. Hopefully, she will find someone who can help her work through the process of healing, and will thus be spared a prolonged period of disturbance in her life.

On the other hand, she may encounter a counselor who will not acknowledge the significance of the abortion episode, thus leaving it unresolved. Or, more commonly, she may simply choose not to deal with it directly. In either case it is likely that she will employ one or more of the following defense mechanisms to protect her from uncomfortable thoughts and feelings:

1. RATIONALIZATION involves finding compelling reasons or excuses for having made the decision to abort. (Example: "It wouldn't have been fair to bring my baby into the world because I wasn't ready to be a mother—I probably wouldn't have been able to be a good mother at this point in my life.")

2. REPRESSION prevents unconscious information

from reaching the conscious mind—blocking out memories of the painful emotions surrounding the abortion. (Example: "I did just fine with my abortion. Sure, I may have been upset a little at the time, but it doesn't bother me at all now.") Sometimes a woman can push down not only the painful emotions but the actual details of the experience as well. Some have even "forgotten" that they had a second or third abortion.

3. COMPENSATION is an effort to make up for the abortion by "doing good things." (Example: being overly involved in church activities, working in the pro-life movement, becoming a "super-mom," having an "atonement baby" soon after the abortion, etc.) It can also mean working very hard to prove that the abortion was really necessary. (Example: if a woman sacrificed her baby for a promising career, she might be heavily invested in making that career a great success.)

4. REACTION FORMATION involves pushing down frightening feelings and thoughts connected with a past abortion by strongly professing the exact opposite of those feelings—as if by expressing the contrary thought enough times, she can begin to believe it. (Example: becoming militantly vocal in the pro-choice movement.)

These defense mechanisms are very effective in keeping the painful memories away, but they consume a lot of a woman's mental energy as she works to suppress powerful emotions. Eventually, if enough stress enters her life, she may find that she lacks the stamina to cope with current stresses *and* continue repressing "forgotten" memories. A variety of experiences (seeing pictures of prenatal development, a subsequent pregnancy, a dentist's drill which resembles the sound of the abortionist's equipment, etc.) may then trigger symptoms associated with Post Abortion Syndrome.

What Are the Symptoms of PAS?

C ounselors who have worked with post-abortion women have seen a wide variety of complaints and emotional problems in their clients. These symptoms will not necessarily appear at the same time, nor is any woman likely to experience all of them. Some may occur immediately after an abortion, and others much later. However, if three or more of the symptoms listed below describe what you have recently experienced in relation to an abortion, it is likely that you are experiencing Post Abortion Syndrome.[1]

GUILT: An individual feels guilt when she has violated her own moral code. For the woman who has come to believe, at some point after an abortion, that she consented to the killing of her preborn child, the burden of guilt is relentless. One can offer little consolation to the woman who has transgressed one of nature's strongest instincts: the protection a mother extends to her offspring.

This inner voice of self-condemnation plays an accusing message in the mind over and over: *You are defective. How could you have done this thing? You are a desperately wicked person*. It is also normal for many post-abortion women entering therapy to verbalize their belief that any unhappy events which have occurred since the abortion were inevitable because they "deserve it." Many of the

---

[1] It is important to remember that an abortion may not be the *only* cause, but a contributor, to these symptoms.

remaining symptoms listed below result from listening to this mental message day in and day out.

ANXIETY: Anxiety is an unpleasant emotional and physical state of apprehension. Post-abortion women with anxiety may experience any of the following: tension (inability to relax, irritability), physical responses (dizziness, pounding heart, upset stomach, headaches), difficulty concentrating, worry about the future, and disturbed sleep.

The conflict between a woman's moral standards and her decision to abort generates much of this anxiety. Very often she will not relate her anxiety to a past abortion, and yet she will unconsciously begin to avoid anything having to do with babies. She may make excuses for not attending a baby shower, skip the baby aisle at the grocery store, and so forth. This unrecognized "baby phobia" may eventually lead to a full-blown agoraphobia, where the mere act of leaving home creates great distress.

• • •

Carol entered therapy a year after her abortion, profoundly shocked at the levels of pain and anxiety she was experiencing. Every day she was taking eight to ten Xanax (a tranquilizer related to Valium) prescribed by a psychiatrist who had discounted her description of the pain surrounding her abortion experience. She had developed agoraphobia and was now in imminent danger of losing her job because of the panic attacks which occurred almost every day prior to leaving for work. Only when she came to realize that her present behavior was somehow connected to her abortion could Carol force herself to drive on the freeway, at night, to attend a post-abortion therapy group.

• • •

PSYCHOLOGICAL "NUMBING": A person who has experienced a highly painful loss will develop an instinct to avoid future situations which might lead to serious pain again. Many post-abortion women maintain a vow, often not verbalized, that they will never again allow themselves to be put in such a vulnerable position. As a result, without conscious thought, they may work hard to keep their emotions on a flat level, experiencing neither highs nor lows. Not only does this flatness of emotional experience affect their own outlook, but it greatly hampers their ability to form and maintain close interpersonal relationships. It is not uncommon during therapy to hear a post-abortion woman talk about her life as if it were happening to another person whom she watches go through all the motions of living.

• • •

Beth described her life this way: "I remember when I was younger I would wake up in the morning excited just to be alive in such a wonderful world. When we first got married things that happened to me either made me really happy or really sad. But after the abortion two years ago, it seemed like something turned off inside me. Nothing touches me anymore, good or bad. I can't get excited about things that used to put me in orbit, and now when I read about sad things that happen in the newspaper, I just think, 'Oh well, life comes and goes. It doesn't really matter. They'll get over it and keep on living.' I wish I could go back to the way I used to be. What's the use of going through life cold and indifferent to things that happen to you and around you?"

43

• • •

DEPRESSION AND THOUGHTS OF SUICIDE: All of us are acquainted with depression. It is a mood filled with sadness, guilt and feelings of hopelessness. A more severe and prolonged depression is characterized by a sense of utter futility, and a complete inability to experience pleasure from any source. It may lead to suicidal ideas, as a woman blames and hates herself so much that she simply wishes she were dead.

Few post-abortion women reach the point of an overt clinical depression. Most continue to function and perform the duties of life, while still experiencing many of the following:

1. SAD MOOD — ranging from feelings of melancholy to total hopelessness.

2. SUDDEN AND UNCONTROLLABLE CRYING EPISODES — the source of which may be a total mystery to the woman if she hasn't yet connected her present sad mood to memories of the abortion. The unpredictability and intensity of these crying spells may give rise to a sense of panic over being so out of control. A more severely depressed person may feel like crying but lack the energy to do so.

3. DETERIORATION OF SELF-CONCEPT — because she feels wholly deficient in her ability to function as a "normal" woman. These feelings of unworthiness are profound because she sees herself as unredeemable—a lost cause. She does not believe she can help herself, nor can anyone else help her.

4. SLEEP, APPETITE, AND SEXUAL DISTURBANCES — usually in a pattern of insomnia, loss of appetite, and/or reduced sex drive. On the other hand, sleeping and eating behaviors can become excessive. (It is unusual, however, for a woman to experience an in-

creased sex drive during a depression. In fact, many post-abortion women report pain with intercourse.)

5. REDUCED MOTIVATION — for the normal activities of life. The things that occupied her life before the depression (working, hobbies, reading, family life, friendships, and so on) just no longer seem worth doing.

6. DISRUPTION IN INTERPERSONAL RELATIONSHIPS — because of the general lack of enthusiasm for all activities. This is especially evidenced in her relationship with her husband or boyfriend, particularly if he was involved in the abortion decision. Anger can be stored against him even if he was "supportive of whatever she decided." A woman is often likely to resent his neutral stand when, in retrospect, she believes he should have been more protective of their child during a time when she herself wasn't thinking clearly. A host of psychosexual disorders crop up in the aftermath of a couple's abortion, and they are far more likely to break up rather than stay together more than one year after the abortion.

7. THOUGHTS OF SUICIDE — or preoccupation with death. Not surprisingly, some post-abortion women are so depressed that they have come to the point of believing they would be better off dead. If such a woman is able to verbalize the desire to end her life, and especially if she actually has a plan to do so, she is experiencing the severest form of clinical depression and needs immediate professional attention.

• • •

Emily described herself, during the first session of a post-abortion therapy group, as being normally a very disciplined person. She was very surprised by her emotional instability over the past several weeks. She said that she was avoiding meals, tossing and turning at night for the first time in her life, and crying in the middle of the day for no reason at all. She had become increasingly irritable with her two children and was easily distracted. (She described one incident where she went into the kitchen to prepare her son's lunch, then found herself standing in the middle of the kitchen, staring off into space, unable to remember what she had started to do.)

Most of all, Emily was terribly frightened because she had never experienced anything like this before. Her husband was becoming angry with her prolonged agitation over the abortion and began to insinuate that maybe she was mentally unbalanced. After many weeks of fighting, Emily had come to feel that it was all quite hopeless and had given up trying to salvage the relationship.

She admitted in that first therapy session that she was toying with the idea of taking her own life but didn't think she could overcome her strong sense of responsibility toward her children. She began to cry profusely as she confessed that even this sense of loyalty to her own children was beginning to crumble. After all, she sobbed, she wasn't a fit mother. Perhaps they would be better off raised by someone else.

• • •

It is important to remember that the symptoms listed above may be seen in *anyone who is depressed.* Post Abortion Syndrome may be the primary cause of the depression, or it may be one of several contributing problems. Some work with an experienced counselor (hopefully one who understands PAS) may be necessary to put all of the components of a depression into perspective.

ANNIVERSARY SYNDROME: There tends to be an

increase of symptoms around the time of the anniversary of the abortion and/or the due date of the aborted child. This phenomenon is reported with some consistency by women who are experiencing PAS.

REEXPERIENCING THE ABORTION: A very common event described by post-abortion women is the sudden onset of distressing, recurring "flashbacks" of the abortion episode. Sometimes this occurs in situations which resemble some aspect of the abortion. A routine gynecological exam is an obvious example, but even the suction sound of a household vacuum cleaner has been reported as a trigger for troubling flashbacks.

Sometimes women report an increase of "happy" baby dreams which leave them sad upon awakening and finding empty arms. More often, however, women re-experience the abortion in the form of recurring nightmares about babies in general or her aborted baby in particular. These dreams usually involve themes of lost, dismembered, or crying babies. One woman described a nightmare in which the bloodied upper torso of her aborted child was clinging to the outside of her bedroom window at night, calling out to her mournfully, "Mommy, help me!" Another woman talked about a nightmare in which she was frantically trying to gather up all the pieces of her aborted baby and put them back together like a jigsaw puzzle. As gruesome as these dreams may sound, they are not unrepresentative of the experiences shared in a post-abortion therapy group.

PREOCCUPATION WITH BECOMING PREGNANT AGAIN: A significant percentage of women become pregnant within one year of their abortion. The desire to become pregnant again—as soon as possible—is verbalized often in the counseling room. This may represent an unconscious hope that a new pregnancy, often called the "atonement baby," will serve as a replacement for the one that was aborted.

ANXIETY OVER FERTILITY AND CHILDBEARING ISSUES: Some post-abortion women maintain a fear that they will never become pregnant again or carry a pregnancy to term. Some expect to have handicapped children because they have disqualified themselves as good mothers. Those women whose worldview includes a belief in God and divine accountability will often verbalize these fears in terms of God punishing them.

DISRUPTION OF THE BONDING PROCESS WITH PRESENT AND/OR FUTURE CHILDREN: The post-abortion woman may not allow herself to become properly bonded to another pregnancy because of a fear of loss, as explained above. Or, she may begin another pregnancy intending to be the "world's most perfect mother" in order to make up for aborting the last pregnancy.

Likewise, the woman who already had children at the time of her abortion may discover that she is beginning to view her existing children in a different light. At one extreme, she may unconsciously "devalue" them. One woman sadly commented, "I always thought my children were the most prized possessions we had; now I catch myself looking at them while they are playing and thinking bizarre things like, 'You were the lucky ones. You were allowed to live.'"

She may go in the opposite direction and become overly protective. Another woman confessed that, since her abortion experience, she had become obsessively involved with her children, wanting to prove to the world and to herself that she was not a bad mother.

SURVIVAL GUILT: Few women abort for trivial reasons. They find themselves in the midst of a heartbreaking situation whereby they stand to lose much if they choose to carry their pregnancies to term. In the end, the decision boils down to a sorrowful conclusion: "It's me or you, and I choose me." In an attempt to assuage the guilt of being the "survivor," a woman will sometimes enter a heightened and unrealistic "compensation mode" whereby she attempts to atone for her choice.

She may keep herself very busy doing volunteer work. Indeed, she may become overly zealous in the pro-life movement. And this, unfortunately, may be the worst possible place for her to be. If she has not found forgiveness for her own abortion, she will not likely be able to extend compassion and forgiveness to anyone else who has aborted. All too often, "talking someone out of having an abortion" becomes her way of making payments on the debt she feels she has. Any seasoned director of a crisis pregnancy center has learned to screen out and refer for counseling the well-intentioned volunteer who hasn't worked through her own abortion. While post-abortion women who have experienced healing and forgiveness are usually highly effective counselors, those who lack the experience of healing can turn a conversation with an abortion-minded woman into a disaster.

DEVELOPMENT OF EATING DISORDERS: Some women seeking post-abortion counseling have developed eating disorders. While this phenomenon remains largely unexplored, several factors may contribute to the correlation between abortion guilt and eating disorders. First, a substantial weight gain or severe weight loss is associated with unattractiveness, which reduces the odds of becoming pregnant again. Second, becoming unattractive serves as a form of self-punishment and helps perpetuate the belief that she is unworthy of anyone's attention. Third, extremes in eating behavior (such as bulimia or anorexia) represent a form of control for the woman who feels her life is otherwise out of control. And finally, a drastic weight loss can shut down the menstrual cycle, thus preventing any future pregnancies.

ALCOHOL AND DRUG ABUSE: Alcohol and drug use often serve initially as a form of self-medication—a way of coping with the pain of the abortion memories. One study found that 78 percent of women alcoholics reported some type of problem related to childbearing, contrasted with 34 percent of the married controls, and it is suggested that gynecologic problems may contribute to doubts a woman has about her own adequacy as a female.[2] Sadly, the woman who resorts to alcohol and/or drugs eventually finds herself having not only more problems but also fewer resources with which to solve them. The mental and physical consequences of alcohol and drug abuse only amplify most of the symptoms the woman is already experiencing.

OTHER SELF-PUNISHING OR SELF-DEGRADING BEHAVIORS: In addition to weight loss and substance abuse, the post-abortion woman may also enter into abusive relationships, become promiscuous, fail to take care of herself medically, or deliberately hurt herself emotionally and/or physically.

• • •

Miriam's mother had originally told her she would support her daughter in whatever decision she made concerning her unplanned pregnancy. But two months after Miriam's abortion, her mother broke down one night, weeping over the abortion, hurling the accusation that "only a slut would sleep around and then callously abort." Already having emotional difficulties with the abortion decision, Miriam slumped

[2] *Association for Interdisciplinary Research in Values and Social Change Newsletter*, Vol. 1, No. 2 (Winter 1988), 2.

into a deep depression. Waitressing at a local restaurant in the evening, she would begin drinking a while before her shift ended, and then go home with whomever looked like the most likely candidate for at least one night of pseudo-closeness. She knew this behavior pattern was self-destructive, but she was willing to do anything to numb the pain of her mother's (and her own) accusations.

• • •

BRIEF REACTIVE PSYCHOSIS: Rarely, a post-abortion woman will experience a brief psychotic episode for two weeks or less after her abortion. The break with reality and recovery are both extremely rapid, and in most cases the person returns completely to normal when it is over. Although an unusual reaction to abortion, it bears mentioning because it is possible for a person to have a brief psychotic reaction to a stressful event without being labeled a psychotic individual. During such an episode, the individual's perception of reality is drastically distorted.

• • •

One single woman, a respected professional who lived by herself in a small town, passed a very large piece of bloody material only hours after returning home after her abortion. She examined it and decided that it had to be her eight-week fetus. (She later reported that the clinic had been extremely busy the Friday she had gone in. Possibly, the physician neglected to make sure the fetus had passed through the suction tube, or perhaps she had been carrying twins.) Because she had, until then, believed that an eight-week fetus is an unidentifiable mass of tissue, the unmistakable human characteristics of the fetus sent waves of horror through her.

Using a soft kitchen towel, she carefully wrapped it up, decided it was a girl, gave her a name, and proceeded to rock her and talk to her during the next two days as if she were a live baby. By late Sunday afternoon, she began to acknowledge that her baby had died. She then drove out to the seaside, because she wanted to "bury" her baby in the ocean. A few hours later, she felt as though she were waking from a long dream. The fetus she passed had been real, but then she had experienced a total break from reality for nearly two days. Needless to say, she was badly shaken by the experience. Having heard that a local crisis pregnancy center offered post-abortion counseling, she came for help soon thereafter. She has not experienced any recurrences of psychotic episodes, brief or prolonged, since that time.

• • •

How Can I Be Healed?

*T*he experiences of many therapists who are now working with post-abortion women show that time alone does not bring real, lasting healing. In fact, frequently the women who are most in need of help are those whose abortions took place years in the past. While a post-abortion woman may have acquired enough coping skills to be a well-functioning member of society, she remains at risk for deterioration if the repressed pain surfaces in some way. When a woman comes to a point in her life where she recognizes the need to deal with a past abortion, a professional or lay counselor can be of great help in leading her through the process of healing, either individually or in a group setting.

Therapists and researchers who have spent countless hours helping women deal with post-abortion pain have consistently found that some basic task areas must be worked through in order for a person experiencing PAS to find relief. The specific *way* in which the work is done may vary considerably, but each task area must be addressed. The ideal approach to dealing with any painful past episode is to involve a second person in the healing process—be it a friend, pastor, lay counselor or professional. The reason for this is obvious: if the event was emotionally painful, the mind has usually worked efficiently to tuck away the hurtful memories into some dark recess of the subconscious so that they will not be disruptive. It's difficult to deal with that negative information on one's own, because the mind automatically seeks to protect mental stability. Another person can gently help a woman bring it into conscious focus where it can be dealt with decisively.

If you feel emotionally wounded from an abortion experience, we hope that this chapter, in particular, will facilitate your healing process, whether or not you can find someone (or a post-abortion support group) to help you. We realize that you may be in an area where there simply aren't many counselors available. It is our prayer that this information will encourage you at least to seek out a trusted friend, preferably someone with some spiritual insight, and share your pain with her.[1]

You may discover that you have already partially worked through one or more of the task areas. It is not uncommon, for instance, for the woman with a Christian worldview to understand (at least on an intellectual level) God's forgiveness, while refusing to admit that she has harbored anger toward those who played a coercive role in her abortion decision.[2] Another woman with no particular religious orientation may fully recognize her

[1]We strongly advise that male friends or lay counselors, even those with the best intentions, avoid working with post-abortion women. The subject matter is difficult, dealing with, among other things, details of sexual experiences which a woman may find awkward to disclose to a man. In addition, some post-abortion women harbor anger toward men (boyfriends, husbands, abortionists, etc.) which may cloud the discussion.

[2]Sometimes, as she observes Christians in the group experiencing God's forgiveness, there arises in a non-Christian woman a yearning for that same reconciliation with her Creator. A Christian counselor needs to be prepared to explain, in the simplest of terms, how to grasp hold of this forgiveness.

We also know that many post-abortion women are not ready to embrace this concept. Here, the counselor must use extreme caution and respect in finding a delicate balance: helping a woman explore spiritual issues while not broadcasting expectations which can become awkward.

anger issues but be totally unaware that she has a spiritual hunger which needs to be addressed. Like every woman who goes through the post-abortion healing process, you will progress through the tasks at different rates, needing to spend a great deal of time with one, and then perhaps finding another relatively easy to work through.

1. Working Through the Denial
(Reexperiencing the Abortion)

The very first task of healing is to access the negative feelings that surrounded the abortion experience. Most women, even those currently experiencing a great deal of post-abortion stress, have utilized repression for so long as a coping strategy that they have long "forgotten" the fear, anger, guilt, and grief associated with the abortion. Until these powerful emotions are fresh in your mind again, there simply is not enough information to work with in order to accomplish the other tasks.

If you are hurting from a recent abortion you are probably thinking, "Are you kidding? There's nothing to 'access'—it's all here, fresh and painful. What I need is an anesthetic; if I *could* submerge it I *would!*" Obviously you haven't had time to employ one or more of the defense mechanisms which others have used for months and years following their abortions. Chances are, however, that the pain you are feeling right now is an *enraged* sort of pain. Your specific goal in this first task area will be to sort out and label the various feelings you are experiencing. You are probably well aware of your anger; but there are other hurts there, as well. Responding to the kinds of questions listed in this section will help you begin.

If your abortion was in the more distant past, the most efficient way to access those feelings is to find a safe, supportive environment in which you can tell your story—whether to a counselor who knows about Post Abortion Syndrome, to a post-abortion support group, or to an understanding friend who is willing to commit a good deal of time to help you.

Since you will naturally tend to avoid something you know will make you feel bad, a sensitive counselor or friend can help you reexperience the abortion, with some gentle prompting to help you persevere in remembering. It may be necessary for you to tell the story more than once, because the more often you are able to verbalize the abortion experience, the more details you will remember.

Here is a beginning list of questions to help you start this process. (Many of these questions have been taken from the excellent post-abortion Bible study by Linda Cochrane. See bibliography for ordering information.) If you are by yourself, make sure you are in a comfortable, private place where you will be uninterrupted for as long as it takes. If you have located a close friend or counselor who is willing to go through this with you, go ahead and write out your answers, and then go over them verbally with that other person.

1. How did you meet the father of the baby?
2. At the time you decided to have sex with him, what was your understanding about the relationship? What do you think his understanding was?
3. Did you ever talk together about the possibility of your sexual activity leading to pregnancy? Was there a mutual understanding as to what course of action would be taken if you got pregnant?
4. What did you feel when you first found out you were pregnant?
5. What was your boyfriend/husband's reaction? Friends' reactions? Parents' reactions? What did they want you to do?

6. What were your feelings about abortion before your pregnancy? Was your decision to abort a violation of your internal sense of "right and wrong"?

7. How did you get to the abortion clinic? How did you feel as you were driving/riding there? What was said? What do you wish had been said?

8. What was it like in the waiting room? Describe the atmosphere around you and what the other patients seemed to be feeling.

9. What did the table feel like? What were you thinking? Did you have second thoughts?

10. How would you describe the clinic workers? Were they understanding and sympathetic? What did you need from them that you didn't get?

11. How did you feel—physically and emotionally—while the abortion was being performed? What did you see? Smell? Hear?

12. How did you feel—physically and emotionally—when it was over?

13. What happened to the relationship with your boyfriend/husband after the abortion? With your parents? With any friend(s) who had an important vote in your abortion decision?

14. What do you think is the most detrimental way abortion has affected your life?

15. If you were in similar circumstances today, would you make the same choice?

It is not unusual to answer these questions in a superficial way the first time you go through them. Your brain is extremely efficient in its ability to avoid confronting information that it knows will hurt, and so it may take a few attempts to access the old feelings. Put your answers away for a few days and then try again. The material you are looking for will have been moved closer to the surface by your earlier efforts. It is extremely common for women going through post-abortion support groups to come back for the second or third session shaken by what they have suddenly remembered since the first telling of their story. (If you are attempting to counsel with a woman experiencing PAS, be very patient with the person who has difficulty accomplishing this first task.)

• • •

Tracy is an attractive professional in her mid-twenties who came to a post-abortion support group after attending counselor training at a local crisis pregnancy center two months previously. She realized that the videos and information on fetal development had caused her a great deal of stress as she remembered her own abortions. She was very surprised at her reaction, because she assumed she had dealt with the issue long ago.

The first session closed as each member took ten minutes to tell the group a little bit about her abortion experience. The women demonstrated varying degrees of sadness or anger, and some shed a few tears. Tracy was the last to share, and the description of her abortions was concise and completely devoid of any emotion. The rest of the group sat in deep compassion as she told of aborting six-month-in-utero triplets when she was fourteen years old. She had spent fourteen hours of labor in a lonely hospital room, waiting to deliver her saline-aborted babies. One year later Tracy was pregnant, and aborted again.

She had never made the connection between these traumatic experiences and the overly controlled manner in which she now conducted her life. After several subsequent attempts to access the emotions of those abortions, Tracy was frustrated. She felt she had come into the group highly motivated to deal with the pain, but she couldn't seem to release the control that now held her back. Eventually, as the counselor had her inject words that conveyed feelings into her story, twelve years of carefully curbed emotions began pouring out, and Tracy could now progress through the rest of the tasks. She is now leading a post-abortion support group in her own town.

• • •

While Tracy's story may seem more dramatic than average, the numbness that had dominated her emotional life is, unfortunately, all too common in the women we see. Anyone who has ever gone through some deeply scarring event understands the indifference that is used to cover hysteria, as well as the tremendous fear of getting in touch with whatever is "down there." Tread gently, and with great compassion, with such a person.

2. Dealing With Issues of Guilt, and Accepting God's Forgiveness

• • •

Jenny came to the crisis pregnancy center in response to a yellow pages ad which offered "post-abortion counseling." In filling out an initial questionnaire about her abortion experience, Jenny listed no particular religious affiliation, either currently or in her family background. Later in the questionnaire, however, she indicated that one of her strongest emotional reactions to the abortion experience was guilt, and feeling "terribly afraid that I've done something against God."

• • •

Maybe you're like Jenny and wonder why you are suddenly thinking about God for the first time in years. Actually, it is very natural for you to be thinking about spiritual things right now, even if you wouldn't ordinarily describe yourself as a "religious" person. It has been our experience in counseling women that very few people really hold a purely atheistic worldview.

Most women have some sort of concept of God and an afterlife, even though definitions differ widely. We think it is important to use this painful place in your life to discover and probably redefine your concept of God. One of our primary convictions in post-abortion counseling is that long-term healing will come only when a woman has been reconciled with God. Those who are able to accept the concept of a personal God, and then ask for and receive his total and unconditional forgiveness, are the women most successful in wiping out their burden of guilt.

The woman with a Christian orientation often has a surprisingly difficult time accepting God's forgiveness for her abortion, whether it occurred before or after her commitment to Christ. If feelings of closeness to God were previously enjoyed prior to the abortion, no such feelings now exist, and she probably believes the relationship to be irreparable in view of her atrocious sin. How dare she presume to sit at his feet like an innocent child after what she has done? Working her way back into the periphery of his kingdom, in the lowest rank of privilege, may be the highest spiritual goal she can imagine.

Many women cannot tolerate these feelings for long

and turn away from the church completely. Others enter into an intense compensation mode, assuming that if they are "good" long enough, if they "prove themselves," God will surely forgive them someday. Of course, this is not a conscious thought process on her part. During therapy, however, a woman may startle herself by realizing that she has had a specific number of years in mind (usually five to seven) for a period of penance.

• • •

Norma was married at twenty-five. When she returned from a one-week honeymoon, she discovered that she was already seven weeks pregnant. In less than twenty-four hours, she, her husband, and her doctor had calmly decided on and carried out an abortion, because they felt this would be a most inopportune time to have a baby.

Norma had been raised in a Christian home with a high regard for life, though she was not a committed Christian at the time of her abortion. This background provoked an internal struggle over the next ten years. For a while she convinced herself that she had been bullied into the decision. But, in fact, the decision had been made calmly and rationally, and eventually she took full responsibility for her choice. She had worked night and day in her church for the last five years since recommitting her life to Christ and still could not begin to consider the idea that she might already be forgiven for the abortion.

One night, during a post-abortion group therapy session, Norma was struggling with the idea of God's forgiveness. The leader asked her to think about what she expected from her young son whenever he did something wrong. "I want him to see the wrong action through my eyes—without denying that he did it or making lame excuses for why he did it," she replied. "And I want to know that he is truly sorry for what he did."

She was perplexed when the counselor asked if she ever remained cold and punishing toward her son once he had reached the point of true repentance. "Why on earth would I do that?" she asked. "He is my child—I love him!" Then she slowly began to realize that God, as her loving parent, had been patiently waiting five years for her simply to turn around and *accept* his forgiveness. She then wept tears of joyous healing.

• • •

The most essential task for the Christian post-abortion woman, then, is to accept, on an emotional level, what she probably already knows on an intellectual level: that God's forgiveness is already complete and that she must reach out and grasp it firmly. There are, in fact, three aspects of forgiveness which are part of this "firm grasp": knowing who ultimately has paid the debt, allowing intimacy with God to be restored, and understanding the difference between punishment and consequences.

The question of debt repayment is illustrated by the story of the unfaithful servant in Matthew 18, who in some ways is like a post-abortion woman seeking to work off her transgression. In this parable a servant asks his master for time to pay back a huge debt, rather than begging to have it forgiven. Unfortunately, the debt equals far more than the servant's entire lifelong earning potential! Similarly, you may have an unspoken notion that you are "doing time" for a past abortion. But how can you ever repay the loss? Like the man in the story, you owe a debt which you can never repay, no matter how long you work!

You cannot put the aborted child back together and give him or her life. You must stop trying to pay the debt and accept the fact that it was paid by Christ's death on the cross two thousand years ago. There is no point in struggling with guilt and repayment. Instead, accept the only gift that brings freedom from guilt.

Restoring intimacy is the second aspect of forgiveness. It is perhaps best understood in our own parent/child relationships. One January a dear artist friend of ours gave us a late Christmas present: a miniature nativity scene which she had carefully sculpted from fragile clay. It was a precious gift, and a unique reminder of the one who made it. I brought it home, set it out on the dining-room table, and told the children about it as I tucked them into bed.

The next morning, however, didn't start out well. Our eleven-year-old son, Chad, was in an uncharacteristically bad mood, looking for a shirt that I hadn't had time to wash. Words he didn't really mean spilled out of his mouth, and I reprimanded him. He flounced angrily down the stairs and I followed, just in time to see him jerk his loaded backpack from the dining-room table. Unfortunately, his backpack swept the beautiful nativity scene onto the floor, with broken arms, halos, and heads flying everywhere. We both stared in silent horror at what remained.

What happened in the next few minutes was a fascinating microcosm of human behavior. Chad's first reaction, as he realized I had witnessed the accident, was to rationalize: "Look what happened! Why did you put that there? It wouldn't have happened if you had put it in a safer place. It's not my fault!" Still stunned by what I had just seen, I didn't yet have the words with which to respond to this absurd protest, so I remained silent. And within a matter of minutes, Chad's useless rationalizations melted as genuine repentance overwhelmed him.

Now, what do I, as a loving parent, want from my child when he has done something wrong? I want for him to see the deed for what it was and to take responsibility for his behavior. Most of all, I need to see genuine sorrow for what he has done. If these are in place, the path to reconciliation is completely cleared. Could I have extended forgiveness to my son if he didn't believe it was his fault? Could I have ignored the situation and expected our relationship to continue on a close and honest level? Of course not. Chad would have carried that guilt around until he finally dealt with it, because it would have created a barrier in our relationship (a highly uncomfortable state of affairs for an eleven-year-old).

And what if, at the point of Chad's genuine repentance, I had responded with harshness, saying cruel things to him to vent the anger I was feeling about my broken nativity scene?[3] What if I had withheld my love and forgiveness until he could earn enough money to replace the broken gift, or until I was satisfied by a long period of "good behavior"? Is this the response of a loving parent? Unfortunately, it is all too often the response of many parents. And it is from our own parents that we form our concept of God as a heavenly parent. For many people, this leads to a very warped idea of how God operates.[4]

One of the most touching illustrations of God's forgiveness is found in the familiar parable of the prodigal

[3]For the sake of historical accuracy, I must confess that, though I did forgive Chad that morning, it took me a full day to work through my feelings of grief and anger over the episode. How grateful I am that God's forgiveness is instantaneous and perfect!

[4]Two excellent books that review the various ways people view God are *Your God Is Too Small*, by J. B. Phillips and *The Father Heart of God*, by Floyd McClung, Jr.

son (Luke 15). After squandering his inheritance, the son eventually finds himself starving in a pig pen. As he remembers his father's benevolence, and the kindness his father showed even the lowliest of servants, he comes to repent of the terrible decisions he has made. Knowing, however, that he doesn't deserve to be received back as a son, he formulates a plan whereby he will return to his father and beg to be hired as a servant.

Meanwhile, the father has been at the gate every day since his son left, hoping and praying that he will return. And now, suddenly, a weary figure trudges toward the estate. In great joy the father receives him back, sparing no expense with the "welcome home" party, and lavishing him with expensive gifts. In response to the son's prepared speech requesting a place among the servants, the father replies, "Nonsense! You are my son, and I am so overjoyed to have you home!"

Have you ever felt like that son? Are you finally at the place where you are ready to stop making excuses and rationalizations as to why you had to have the abortion? Do you just want to "go back home," longing for the days before all this pain started? Maybe, like the son, you have written off the possibility of enjoying a close relationship with God, but would be happy just to be "in the camp." We have heard women verbalize that they would be content if they could just be allowed to participate on the periphery, like a foot soldier who is unknown to the general but still part of the army.

Have you felt that you didn't deserve a special, personal relationship with God, that you didn't deserve to call him "Abba" ("Dad")? That feeling of self-condemnation does not come from God, who stands "by the gate" every day waiting for you to come home.

Finally, as you are dealing with the pain of ongoing memories you may be confusing the consequences of your abortion with punishment. In the story of the prodigal son, there was no punishment given by the father. On the other hand, neither could he magically create a new endowment for his son. Although the relationship was completely restored, the son had to live for the rest of his life knowing that he had wasted his inheritance money. The father could soften that blow somewhat by providing for him, but the squandered fortune was gone.

If you are a parent, you can probably think of a time when your child made an irresponsible decision that brought consequences you would have liked to reverse but were powerless to do so. Our daughter Carrie once took our extremely tame but dim-witted cockatiel out of his cage in the back yard. She believed that he would be content to stay on her shoulder as he always had while in the confines of the house. But when this bird felt the sunshine on his shoulders, he was history! He soared on unclipped wings to freedom, and we never saw him again.

Was Carrie genuinely sorry for taking the bird out of the cage? Absolutely. She fully understood the foolishness of her action. She was brokenhearted and her remorse continued for months after the incident. And as heartsick as I was for Carrie, there was utterly nothing I could do to bring that blasted bird back. Carrie begged forgiveness for letting him out, and the family forgave her instantly, but she had to live with the painful consequences of that action for a very long time.

God, as a loving parent, is as grieved over your abortion choice as you now are. He feels your pain and has no desire to make you suffer more than you already have. What you have experienced is not a punishment from him, and hopefully it will not separate you from him.

There are many women who, though coming to understand the loving, forgiving nature of God, are seemingly unable to move through this important second task. To trust fully is a frightening proposition for someone who has never experienced the joy of a trusting relationship with a father (or any other man, for that matter). Additionally, some women unconsciously choose not to accept God's forgiveness. Holding on to one's "defectiveness" can become a rationalization for failing to move forward as a new, whole, healthy person who is responsible for her present behavior. It may be time for you to leave behind your shroud of reasons why you are such a "bad," defective person and instead decide to believe what God has said about his ability to forgive whatever you've done and make you whole.

3. Anger and Forgiveness Toward Self and Others

Most women experiencing Post Abortion Syndrome have been suppressing a tremendous amount of anger since the time of the abortion. Usually they will resist getting in touch with this dark emotion and identifying it for what it is. Sometimes this is caused by a fear that expressing anger will lead to rage and then a total loss of control. The Christian woman is often especially hampered in this task area, because she has heard countless sermons exhorting her not to harbor resentment toward another human being, but rather to forgive others as she has been forgiven by Christ.

The biblical command to forgive others as we have been forgiven is an abiding truth. Unfortunately, until we can identify precisely what needs to be forgiven, it lays beneath the surface like a pool of toxic waste material, ever threatening to bubble up and poison our desperate striving for wholeness. The post-abortion woman must stop denying the pain and anger she felt (and feels) before, during, and after her abortion. Recognizing anger clears the path to genuine and permanent forgiveness.

• • •

Elisa's mother and father had coerced her into getting an abortion when she was fifteen years old. In the post-abortion therapy group, she denied, sweetly, any traces of bitterness against her parents, even though they had refused to discuss the episode with her over the years. As an adult, she knew that what they had done was wrong, but she believed that, as a Christian, she had no grounds for harboring any resentment toward them.

She shocked herself when she was asked to write a pretend letter to God telling him how she felt about her mother's part in the abortion decision. The rage she expressed in writing distressed her greatly, because she honestly didn't know where it had come from. As she began talking about the contents of the letter in group one night, she slowly realized that the anger she had unconsciously held against her parents all these years had created a tremendous rift in her relationship with them.

That night she made a conscious decision to stop blaming them for the abortion, and the path to true forgiveness was opened wide. She had a long talk with her parents before the group ended and joyously described to us the tears of reconciliation that were shared between the three of them. They had wanted, for years, to explain to her that their motivation for urging her to get an abortion had been love and concern for her future. Realizing their horrible mistake, they had wanted to talk to her about their failure but had been unable to bring themselves to the point of addressing the issue.

• • •

Part of the work in this task area involves not only admitting that the anger is there, but also deciding what kind of anger you are holding. The kind of anger in which you blame everyone and everything for your abortion, absolving yourself from taking any responsibility, is unjustified. Are you willing to be unhappy and miserable for the rest of your life because of someone else's actions? (This "someone else" could be a person who is long gone and wouldn't even remember your name now.)

A different, more useful kind of anger says, "I can take responsibility for my choice, recognizing that those who should have been the most helpful during this time in my life actually assisted me in making a decision that ultimately hurt me." The difference is in the concept of shared blame. As long as you refuse to admit any responsibility for the abortion, you will always be the perennial victim, who cannot control anything that happens to you. When you finally come to the point of acknowledging your responsibility and accepting forgiveness, your happiness and wholeness no longer depend on anyone else's bad choices. And you are suddenly free to forgive others who were involved.

An important part of this task is identifying those who are the targets of your anger. The possibilities could include the father of the aborted baby, a parent, a close friend, the abortionist, yourself, or God. And sometimes your anger can be directed at someone who had nothing to do with your abortion at all—such as a current boyfriend or husband.[5]

[5] Women who come into a post-abortion group often express frustration and anger when their husband/boyfriend does not support their attending the group. If the husband/boyfriend was the father of the aborted baby, he may have his own post-abortion issues with which to

A good beginning exercise in this task area might be to list all of the people who had anything to do with your abortion experience and write a letter that begins,

"Dear God:

I am angry with _____ because . . . "

Often a woman will be angry at someone, not for promoting the abortion decision, but for taking the ever popular stand, "I'll support you in whatever you decide to do." Many women in the post-abortion support groups have expressed deep and bitter resentment against a boyfriend or husband who thought he was doing the modern thing by letting the choice be hers, when instead she desperately wanted him to say, "This is our baby— the product of our love. We'll make this work somehow." She feels he should have been strong at a time when she was most vulnerable, and her hostility runs deep.

• • •

During the first session of the group, Jolene quietly described her abortion of thirteen years ago, involving a young man to whom she had been engaged. When she became pregnant, she automatically assumed they would simply move the wedding date up, but he argued vehemently for an abortion. Numbed with shock, she gave in rather than gamble on his walking out on the relationship.

deal. He may resent the fact that his wife/girlfriend is "stirring the pot" again by deliberately focusing on an episode he would prefer to be forgotten. If the husband/boyfriend was *not* the father of the aborted baby, he may feel resentful that his wife/girlfriend wants to spend time in a group where she is going to discuss her prior sexual relationship with another man.

Two weeks before the wedding, he walked anyway. Three years later Jolene married another man with whom she now enjoys a fair relationship. They have wanted to have children, but Jolene has miscarried twice.

In response to the group's outraged questions about her feelings toward the father of the child she aborted, Jolene stated that she had never felt any anger toward him. The group sat back in disbelief. Three sessions later, after working on the anger chapter in the *Women in Ramah* workbook, she confessed that there might be some residual anger after all. And by the time she got to the assignment of writing a pretend letter, her wrath had grown to volcanic proportions. She spent an hour one night during the group vomiting up the foul feelings she had harbored against him for the past thirteen years.

The sheer magnitude of her anger was frightening to Jolene, who had spent so many years denying that it even existed. What she hadn't realized was that her anger toward the faithless fiancé had seriously impaired her ability to form a close, trusting relationship with her husband. By the time the group had ended, she had released forever the anger toward her old boyfriend, started marriage counseling with her husband, and experienced tremendous growth in their relationship.

· · ·

It is interesting that sometimes a post-abortion woman can extend compassion toward other members of the therapy group but be unable to forgive herself. Pointing out the inconsistency between her behavior and her thinking, coupled with the understanding and compassion she feels from the rest of the group, will often help a woman relinquish her entrenched self-recrimination.

. . .

Liza met her husband while he was still in the midst of divorce proceedings. She became pregnant but did not tell him for fear of putting too much pressure on him during a time in his life that was already too stressful. Because it was 1956, Liza performed an illegal abortion on herself by inserting a sharp instrument through her cervix. She almost bled to death before finally getting to a hospital, where a physician angrily completed the botched abortion, verbally abusing her during the procedure for attempting such a stupid thing. A staunch Catholic, Liza was deeply ashamed of what she had done and never told anyone about it until she entered a post-abortion therapy group thirty-one years later.

She put off telling her story to the group as long as possible. When she finally did start talking, she could not bring herself to reveal that she had actually tried to abort herself. After much gentle urging from the counselor, she finally blurted out her confession and put her hands over her face, waiting for the condemnation she knew would come. To her great surprise, the other women silently wept in sorrow for the turmoil she must have felt to be driven to such a desperate act and for the burden she had carried alone for so many years. For Liza, the fact that these women were readily able to love her, no matter what she had done in the past, was a major turning point in her being able to forgive herself.

. . .

As a last word of caution, it is important to keep in mind the purpose of this task area. The purpose is *not* to create anger and bitter resentment where none previously existed. The purpose is *not* to have a "primal scream" type of therapy session in which everyone shouts obscenities at people who are no longer around. The purpose is to understand that unacknowledged anger allows us to keep blaming others for our failures. As soon as we see the anger for what it is, and to whom it is directed, we begin to understand our need to forgive the other person.

In almost every post-abortion group, this question comes up: "Should I go to _____ and tell him/her that I have forgiven them?" There is no black-and-white answer to that question. You must ask yourself, "What is my motivation for telling this person? What do I think can be gained?" If you haven't had contact with the father of your baby for some time, chances are he doesn't really care about the forgiveness you're extending him. Such an exercise would be futile at best, and perhaps even destructive. On the other hand, if the father of your baby is someone with whom you have had ongoing contact, and the pain between you has never stopped, by all means this is probably the time to talk to him about this.

If you feel "stuck" in this task area and can't seem to release the anger you feel toward someone, perhaps you have come to the point where you must ask what you are "buying" with that anger. Is it scary to think about living as a whole, responsible person, without making excuses for your bad choices because of the way someone else victimized you? Or perhaps you feel that becoming a whole person would be disloyal to your aborted child. Perhaps feeling ugly and angry toward yourself and others is part of your "penance." If you have an emotional reaction to any of these statements, you need to consider the possibility that something inside of you needs to hold on to that damaged self-concept. Remember, if God has forgiven you, what basis do you now have for withholding forgiveness from yourself? And if you have forgiven yourself, what basis do you now have for withholding forgiveness from anyone else?

4. Grieving the Loss of the Aborted Child

Anyone who has lost a loved one knows how woefully inadequate are the comments from those who have never suffered a loss: "Well, at least he's with the Lord now." "Aren't you glad she won't be in pain anymore?" Friends flock around the bereaved one with sympathetic attention . . . for about two to four weeks. After that, life is supposed to be resumed as always.

For those who experience pregnancy loss through miscarriage, prenatal death, or stillbirth, the litany of thoughtless remarks is worse: "It's just as well, honey; miscarriage is the body's way of rejecting a defective fetus." "Good thing you're young—you've got lots of time to have as many children as you want." "Aren't you glad you didn't carry it any longer than you did?" And the time of mourning (especially for the woman who miscarries early in the pregnancy) is callously reduced to the time needed to recuperate physically. The person who has never lost a pregnancy cannot begin to understand that a woman who has lost one will carry around a little hole in her heart for the rest of her life.

For those who have lost a child through abortion, the public awareness of the need to grieve the loss is utterly nonexistent. The woman herself usually cannot identify that need. Hindering her in this important task of healing are (1) the belief that, as the one who decided on the abortion, it would be hypocritical for her to presume to mourn the baby's death, (2) the fact that she has no memories of a whole child to facilitate a healthy grieving process, and (3) societal denial of the need to grieve what was, after all, only a "lump of pregnancy tissue."

It is crucial for a post-abortion woman to come to the understanding that she aborted a baby. Unlike the mother who has lost a two-year-old, the post-abortion woman has no memories of her child. And since a healthy grieving process requires those warm sensory memories, it is often necessary to help a woman "re-create" her baby—pretending she knows his or her physical characteristics in order to plant a mental and emotional picture firmly in her mind.[6] Naming the child also seems to be an important task, because it gives her child individuality.

With a portrait now indelibly etched on her heart, she can begin the difficult task of asking her child's forgiveness for the abortion. This can be a very frightening experience for the Christian woman who pictures her child now standing next to God, stretching an accusing finger down toward earth. This picture, of course, adds to her feelings of alienation from God. A woman must come to realize that nobody in God's presence could reflect anything but his love, compassion, and forgiveness.[7] After an emotional and tender reconciliation with the child

---

[6] An issue that seems to come up with some regularity in the counseling room is the question of the current developmental stage of the child. Should she think of him or her as a preborn fetus, a newborn baby, the age he/she would now be, or an adult? While most women progressing through this task naturally prefer to think in terms of a small baby, it is important for her to understand that, no matter what the child looks like physically, he or she certainly has the same perceptual awareness of an adult at this point. See 1 Corinthians 15:35–44.

[7] We cannot recommend strongly enough the book *Tilly* by Frank Peretti to help a woman work through this task area. Focus on the Family produced a dramatization of this story on audio cassette which is equally moving (see bibliography for ordering information).

she never knew, after she feels that her child has already forgiven her, she will finally be in a position to say goodbye to her baby . . . for now.

It cannot be overstated that the purpose of this process is *not* to have a woman attempt to communicate with her dead child in some way. She should understand this very clearly. Furthermore, the imagining of the child's characteristics does not presume that she is contacting an "inner guide" from her subconscious mind. Also, the imagination process is not intended to manipulate external reality in any way. Rather, this is a technique to help a woman express her feelings about a real child—a necessary part of the grieving process. In addition, this exercise helps a woman gain a clear understanding of where her children are, and what their relationship will be some day when they are reunited.

A wonderful technique to help her facilitate this step is to encourage her to write a pretend letter to her aborted child, pouring out her heart and explaining (but not excusing) the circumstances under which the abortion was obtained. She might tell the child how much he or she is missed, how sorry she is, how she longs to see him or her someday, and so forth. Here is an actual letter (edited):

"Dearest Baby:
I don't know how to begin writing this letter to you. I hope it's okay to think of you as a girl, because I always believed in my heart you were. You know, I only had your two brothers after I was pregnant with you, and I always wanted a daughter. I would have named you Dawn, and when I picture you, I see you with brown curls tied up in pigtails with pretty ribbons, and big, big blue eyes, just like mine. . . . Baby Dawn, what can I say to tell you how sorry I am that I don't have you to hug or to dress or to put ribbons in your hair? I was so young and frightened when I found out you were growing inside of me. I

allowed some foolish people to talk me into killing the only daughter I ever had, and I have to live with that for the rest of my life. . . . I'm so happy you're with Jesus now. For a long time now heaven has seemed like a really scary place to me because I was afraid of seeing you again, but lately I've begun to understand that you understand and have forgiven me. I can't wait to hold you one day. Goodbye, my precious daughter . . . "

How Do I Live
With the Memories?

*H*aving successfully worked through these major task areas, will you ever feel pain over your abortion again? Most likely. It is unrealistic to expect that someone who has grieved deeply will never again come up against painful reminders of her loss. The goal is for you to become a whole, functioning person who is able to cope with those ongoing reminders when they arise, rather than feeling overwhelmed by them.

Many times, while lecturing on this subject around the country, I have met women during a break who ask fearfully, "How do I know if I've been healed from my abortion experience? I thought I had dealt with it pretty well two years ago, and I'm really surprised at how emotional I've become while listening to you today. I came here because I thought I was ready to run a post-abortion support group, but now I'm having real doubts. Have I just been kidding myself?"

A woman who has worked diligently through all the task areas of healing may be upset when some old and confusing feelings suddenly confront her. Most often she will question whether the work she completed earlier was legitimate. (Because this occurs so often during seminars on Post Abortion Syndrome, we now address this issue at the beginning of any talk.)

Sometimes a return of symptoms may indicate that you need to complete one or more of the task areas. For instance, I have worked with many women who seemed

to have dealt successfully with issues of guilt and forgiveness, but who never recognized their deep need to grieve
the loss of their aborted child. I have talked to other
women who have been completely uninhibited about
mourning their loss, but who have harbored a deep-
rooted bitterness against those who pushed them toward
the abortion. If you have only partially worked through
the task areas; it is understandable that you will feel
anxious and fearful as you approach uncharted territory.

It has often been observed that Americans live in an
"instant" society. This cultural expectation for immediate
results extends, unfortunately, into the universe of those
who grieve. So it is natural that the woman who has
finally faced the pain of a past abortion, worked through
the tasks, and experienced substantial healing will be
bewildered at the first sign of returning painful memories.
"Once healed, always healed" is a fantasy. In reality, the
painful memories may return again and again.

One of the most important gifts a counselor can give
to the woman who has just spent weeks and perhaps
months working through her abortion pain is an understanding of the healing process. A simple analogy may
help clarify this.

Imagine for a moment that your mind is a beautiful
oak roll-top desk in a California home on the San Andreas
fault. Hurriedly stuffed into dozens of small slots and
pigeonholes in that desk are all your ugly abortion
memories because you needed desperately for your
desktop to look clean. As months and years passed, you
continued to stuff the slots with life's disappointments
and pain. Now it takes quite a bit of effort to cram
anything else into the desk.

Suddenly a large earthquake erupts, and all of the
contents of those dark pigeonholes are mercilessly thrown
all over the desk. What a mess! Can you stuff them back

into the holes? Suppose you decide to go through the agonizing process of sorting through the entire, chaotic pile. One by one you pick up bits and scraps of long-forgotten feelings and deal with them, thoughtfully deciding where each item belongs. Now your desktop is not only neat, but the "hidden" parts of your desk are completely organized and dealt with.

But, as every Californian knows, after a major earthquake comes a series of aftershocks. So half of what you labored so hard to organize comes tumbling back onto the desktop. This time, though, it doesn't take nearly as long to recover from the situation. You now know where everything belongs and the process of restoring order will not take as long.

In just the same way, the person who has gone through the painful process of sorting out the guilt, fear, anger, and grief of an abortion is going to experience "aftershocks." When they occur, you must deal immediately with the feelings that are reemerging. The work has been done before, so it's not going to be as traumatic, nor should it cause as much disruption in your life as the initial "quake" (unless there remains a task area which has not been explored).

There will always be ongoing events that trigger one or more of the painful abortion memories. You will probably always remember the anniversary of your abortion and/or the baby's original due date. Everywhere you will be confronted with prenatal pictures, baby commercials, pregnant friends, and playing children. You will never forget the child that was never born, and sometimes the pain will be worse than at other times. As in any grieving process, the painful days will eventually become farther and farther apart, and the memories less upsetting. But this may take longer than our society, with its fixation on the "instant" solutions, is usually prepared to allow any grieving person.

Even though aftershocks may be a problem, there are also some observable characteristics that may indicate that someone has experienced substantial healing from PAS:

1. There is a rapid decrease in symptoms as she resumes normal functioning in her life. Not only does she "pick up where she left off" before the increasing symptoms brought paralysis into her routine, but she should be functioning at a higher level because her ability to maintain close, personal relationships will have improved. Having confronted the role of denial in her life, she is now more honest in dealing with her feelings, and thus has greater ability to communicate with those closest to her (spouse, boyfriend, children, parents, friends).

• • •

Gina, thirty-two, had been married ten years but had never told her husband about the abortion she had when she was fifteen. One of the greatest fears in her life was that her husband would no longer love her in the same way if he knew she had consented to an abortion. So she chose not to reveal her secret. But as the years passed and the stresses of life piled up, Gina began resenting a relationship built on the conditional love she imagined her husband to have for her. ("I love you only because you are so wonderful," she imagined him saying.) The longer this continued, the more Gina decided that her husband was incapable of handling the truth.

Balanced dangerously between an irrational but growing disappointment with her husband and an unwillingness to test his love by telling him, many areas of her life became increasingly disrupted, until she finally sought help through a post-abortion group. Over time, the group helped her through one of the hardest tasks of her life: confiding in her husband about her previous abortion. His understanding and compassionate response dispelled all of her preconceived beliefs about how he would react, and their marriage relationship today is built on an honesty they had never previously enjoyed. Because of that healed relationship, Gina's capacity for dealing with the normal routines of life has been greatly enhanced.

• • •

2. She can speak openly about her abortion experience when it is appropriate to do so. There is nothing quite so touching as a woman who can talk about her abortion and subsequent healing without being afraid of what people might think. This is the woman who has been set free by the knowledge that her slate has been wiped completely clean. The exhilaration of this heart knowledge is so powerful that it completely eclipses any former fear of someone learning her deep, dark secret.

To balance this statement, it should be pointed out that most women who have gone through the healing process will not choose to address large groups on the topic of their abortion. (Indeed, the pro-life community must be careful to guard against exploiting these women by pressuring them to speak at public functions.) If a woman seems to demonstrate a compulsive need to address groups in order to give excruciating details of her abortion experience, she may be trying to "do penance" through this repeated verbal self-abuse. The woman who has experienced healing will find herself willing (though not necessarily eager) to share her story in any situation where she judges the hearer(s) will benefit from her narrative.

3. She uses owning, non-blaming language when talking about the abortion. Because she has stopped rationalizing her abortion, the woman who has known healing can simply admit she made a wrong choice for which she has experienced total forgiveness. There is no trace of accusation (toward herself or others) in her tone of voice or description of what happened to her.

• • •

Darlene was fourteen years old when a close friend of the family sexually abused her, convincing her it would be useless to tell anyone because "no one believes kids—they lie and exaggerate." Over the next four years, Darlene became heavily involved with drugs and overeating. When she became pregnant, her "boyfriend" blamed her for the pregnancy, informed her she would have to pay for the abortion, and disappeared. She was married and divorced within one year of her abortion.

Darlene's life became a downward spiral of drugs, drinking, promiscuity, and self-hatred. The merry-go-round ended with an overdose of tranquilizers and an eighteen-hour coma in the hospital's intensive care unit. Realizing finally that she had hit bottom, Darlene started attending church for the first time in many years. She heard about post-abortion counseling offered in a local center and attended group sessions.

Today she is involved in helping other post-abortion women work through the healing process. One of the highlights of watching these women enjoy wholeness again is witnessing a soft-spoken, beautiful young woman like Darlene speak publicly about her experience in a very straightforward manner, without anger and without blame.

. . .

4. She accepts God's unconditional and total forgiveness. She is also able, finally, to stop hating herself and to extend forgiveness and/or understanding toward others who assisted and supported her abortion decision. She has completely relinquished any traces of doubt that she is forgiven, entirely and eternally. She has stopped playing the accusing mental "tapes" which told her that she would never be absolved of such a hideous crime. Having grasped the beautiful reality of forgiveness, she finds it difficult to hold on to any grudges toward others.

She now understands that the burden of guilt for anyone else who was involved is an issue which will have to be resolved by that person alone. Nothing she can do will affect how another person will process the abortion (except, when appropriate, letting the other know of her own healing experience and of her forgiveness and release of that person).

5. She feels reconciled with her aborted child. For the Christian woman this is an especially important indication of her inner healing, because she knows she will meet her child again someday. If she expects their reunion to be painful, or if she cannot be assured that her child is whole and happy and at perfect peace, then the prospect of life and relationships after death will be terrifying. But the woman who has accepted all of God's forgiveness through Christ can look forward with wistful anticipation to being reunited with her child and is now free to enjoy a close relationship with God during the rest of her earthly life.

6. She is able to deal successfully with the ongoing memories. When the "aftershocks" come rolling through, and she fears she will once again be lost in the damaging emotions, she is able to recover her balance fairly quickly. She can tell herself, "I'm *not* that scared little girl anymore; I've worked through all that, and I'm whole now." And on those days when the emotions are inevitable (anniversary dates, etc.), she can give herself permission to take a short time out to be alone, knowing she will not be consumed by emotions which are out of control.

• • •

Before concluding this chapter, we would like to add a postscript to Linda's story, which we told at the beginning of this book.

After two more months of depression, Linda called a crisis pregnancy center located in her community. A concerned friend had told her that one of the services offered by the center was post-abortion counseling. She attended the initial session of a therapy group one night. Although the first meeting had been previously defined as primarily informational, Linda cried several times during the two-hour session.

Four sessions into therapy, Linda became a Christian through the efforts of the friend who had recommended her to the center. Between her deepening commitment to Jesus Christ and time spent in the group, she began pulling together the pieces of her life and looking at them to figure out how she had arrived at her present situation. Her depression and late-night outbursts had decreased. When the group ended several weeks later, Linda had managed to stabilize her daily mood swings. And, finally, she was able to begin making plans for a family.

How Can I Help Other Women?

Guidelines for Post-abortion
Support Groups

We have included this chapter primarily in response to the people who have called from all parts of the country urgently requesting information about running post-abortion support groups. Ideally, those who wish to start such a group should make arrangements for some formal training through one of the national organizations that are experienced in this area.[1] There are, however, situations in which the need is immediate and the logistics of receiving training are difficult. We thus offer (with several cautions) the following basic guidelines for setting up a post-abortion support group.[2]

While a number of qualified organizations offer manuals to use in a group setting, we use and will refer to the *Women in Ramah* workbook (see bibliography for ordering information). However, the information offered here is applicable to any post-abortion support group, regardless of the particular manual being used.[3]

[1] We are involved with the PACE (Post Abortion Counseling and Education) program and highly recommend it. Names and addresses of the Christian Action Council (which operates the PACE program) and other organizations which offer training are listed at the end of this book in a section titled "Where to Find Help."

[2] This is by no means the only way to structure a post-abortion support group. It is, however, the format Teri has used in the past four years and has a proven track record.

[3] Those of us who are pioneers in this field and who are creating materials to help women suffering from Post Abortion Syndrome are not competing in any way. (This is why we listed so many organizations at

The Group Setting

Although many professionals prefer individual counseling, the group setting is an ideal medium for the lay counselor for a number of reasons.

First, hope is born in the very first meeting, as the women come together for the first time and see others who are also dealing with this problem. (*Wow! I thought I was the only one going crazy from a past abortion. Look at her . . . she looks so normal . . . could she be as stressed out as I am about this?*) A majority of women suffering from PAS have kept their "deep, dark secret" to themselves for so long that they don't realize how many other women in their own community are also suffering. An immediate bonding takes place in the first session simply because they share the same secret.

Second, each woman who starts in a post-abortion support group is at a different place on what has been called the "coping-collapsing continuum."[4] Yet while there will be distinctions between them (in personality type, socioeconomic background, etc.), the group members will develop a sense of "we-ness" as they help each other along. Eventually the trust that evolves among members becomes therapeutic in itself. As each woman finally feels safe and accepted by the group, her self-concept is strengthened immeasurably. After all, the group leader is *supposed* to be sympathetic; to be validated by the rest of the women is far more meaningful.

Another advantage of the group setting is that it

the end of this book.) In fact, as we have come together at conferences and professional symposiums, we have been gratified to discover the similarities in our findings. We may organize the material differently, but we are in agreement as to the basic tasks of healing.

[4] Irving D. Yalom, *The Theory and Practice of Group Psychotherapy* (New York: Basic Books, Inc., 1975), 6.

allows each member the freedom to do as much or as little work as she chooses in a given session. She is permitted to progress at her own rate. A woman who has not focused her attention directly on the abortion episode for many years will not be able to share immediately. It is critical to let each member speak only when she is ready to do so, and the group setting grants her this safeguard.

Additionally, a member may gain an important insight within a span of fifteen to thirty minutes and then need to process this new information quietly as another member "takes the ball." Usually when one woman makes a profound breakthrough in one of the task areas, the other women are "tailgating" on her insight, simultaneously applying her new understanding to their own situations. Consequently the therapeutic effect in a group setting is multiplied.

Finally, as each woman begins to relax in the warm confidentiality, acceptance, and trust of the group, she is able to drop her guard and be herself. The group members, abiding by strict ground rules (which are monitored by the leader), give an important array of reactions and feedback to each other. They help correct false and unrealistic thinking and offer real hope for ultimately working through the pain.

Should I Be Facilitating a Group Like This?

Before becoming involved in this type of effort, it is important to review your own motivation, capabilities, and resources:

1. Do you feel definitely "called" to lead a post-abortion support group, or are you feeling pressured into it because no one else will do it, or because others feel you are the most logical person for the job? If you do not have a strong and sustained interest in becoming involved in this kind of group, by all means don't start one!

2. Do your co-workers, spiritual leaders, and trusted friends believe you are the person for this job? If your "calling" has not been confirmed by those who know you best, you are probably not the right person.

3. How does your family (especially spouse and children) feel about you leading a group? Will another night out be disruptive to your family? And more importantly, if you have had an abortion yourself, are your immediate and extended families ready to have that fact revealed to others? Leading a post-abortion support group can be extremely draining, and it is important that you have a lot of backing from family members.

4. Do you have previous counseling experience? This can include lay counseling experience (as a volunteer at a crisis pregnancy center, a hospice worker, a suicide or rape hotline counselor, etc.). We unequivocally advise that you have counseling experience before attempting to lead a group like this.

5. Have you experienced a substantial healing of your own grief and guilt issues? This applies to any hurtful episode in your life and is especially important if you have had a previous abortion.[5] We have talked to women who are attempting to work on their own pain by leading a group, and this can be extremely damaging to the participants. In many areas, several women who were

[5]During seminars, many women have asked if it is necessary to have had a previous abortion before attempting to lead a post-abortion support group. While it is obviously an asset to have experienced healing from your own painful abortion memories, you are not at all disqualified from this work if you have not had an abortion.

You will be a more effective group leader, however, if you have experienced healing from some type of significant painful episode in your life—the death of a loved one, an extra-marital affair (yours or your spouse's), bankruptcy, betrayal by a trusted friend, etc. From these trials you can draw memories which will help you to understand what the post-abortion woman is experiencing.

interested in leading groups have first gone through the study together, to be certain they have experienced healing in the different task areas before attempting to help other women with their pain.

6. Are you comfortable with strong displays of emotions? Sometimes women who are working through the anger and pain of a past abortion can become distraught. This is especially true if you have succeeded in creating an environment in which each participant feels safe making herself vulnerable to the rest of the group. If a woman unleashes a strong display of emotion and you appear uncomfortable, she will sense this immediately and withdraw, feeling that she has made a fool of herself. Indeed, she may not return to the group at all.

7. Are you willing to be transparent and vulnerable in a group setting? Do you envision yourself being the expert who is going to help these women from an emotional distance, or are you willing to share with the group *your* past pain and healing process?

8. What are your own basic assumptions about women who have aborted? If you have not forgiven yourself for having an abortion, or if you have never had an abortion, you may have a judgmental attitude toward those who abort, without even realizing it. Every good counselor knows there are certain issues he or she does not handle well (and should refer to someone else) because of personal biases.

9. Are you willing to do whatever it takes to gain a basic skill proficiency? Starting with the bibliography and resources listed at the back of this book, you must be willing to learn as much as you can about Post Abortion Syndrome, grieving, and the group process. Being a lay counselor does not excuse you from being knowledgeable.

10. Do you have liability coverage and professional backing? If you are a lay counselor, it would be wise to conduct your post-abortion support group under the auspices of some organization which will provide liability coverage for you as a trained lay counselor.

Additionally, we cannot emphasize strongly enough the need for you to develop a good relationship with one or more qualified professional counselors who are familiar with Post Abortion Syndrome. You will get in over your head with some clients, and it is critical that you have easy access to at least one professional with whom you can consult at any time about situations arising within the group. The best arrangement is to find someone who is willing to meet with you on a weekly basis to check your progress. This kind of expert "backup" can be a source of great comfort to the lay counselor who is struggling with challenging problems.

Screening a Potential Group Participant

Not every woman who requests help is a candidate for a post-abortion group. A short (twenty to thirty minutes) individual screening session between the leader and each potential group member is advisable. She should provide a very brief account of her history and current issues. (It is important that the details and emotions be saved for the group, as much as possible.)

Be aware of situations which might suggest that someone is not going to do well in a group setting. There are also indicators that a potential group member should be referred to a professional, and/or that you should see her individually, rather than as a group participant. Never be afraid to admit that you are not sufficiently trained to counsel everyone who comes to you for help.

1. Is she so depressed that she might be suicidal? Every counselor, professional or not, should be competent to detect suicidal thinking. As a lay counselor, you are not equipped to treat clinical depression, but you need enough knowledge to identify when a woman is depressed so severely as to require professional help before she enters the group. *If at all possible, refer her to a counselor who understands PAS.* If no such professional exists in your community, find one who at least is open and willing to review the information you can provide.

2. Are there too many issues surfacing at once? If, in your judgment, the woman has too many ongoing conflicts (for example, recent divorce, death in the family, substance abuse problem at home, trouble with teenagers) which seem to be competing for equal time in her emotional life, she should probably be referred to a professional counselor, who will help her prioritize the work she needs to do. A woman who is grappling with too many issues at once will dominate group time and overwhelm other members.

3. Does she have an alcohol/substance abuse problem? Any woman who has an alcohol/substance addiction is so adept at denial that it will be extremely difficult for her to maintain the honesty required to work through the task areas in a group. Sadly, many women who have had abortions (or experienced any other event that has caused much pain) turn to alcohol and/or drugs as a form of self-medication. Treating addictions is a difficult process which should be handled by a trained professional— hopefully (as stated previously) one who understands how an abortion figures into the present problem. If the abortion is considered inconsequential (as it so often is in the professional community), the therapist will only treat the symptom (the addiction) without working on what may have been the primary reason for beginning the addiction (the abortion).

4. Is there a history of psychological problems? As part of your screening interview, you need to find out if the woman has ever been hospitalized for mental illness, taken any kind of prescription medication for emotional stress, or been treated by a professional counselor at any time during her life. If she has, she is probably out of your "league" if you are a lay counselor.

On the other hand, one who has gone to a counselor to help deal with some issues in life is not automatically a "mental case" who cannot fit into your group. (Indeed, she may be in better condition than someone who has resisted seeking any kind of help in the past.) Ultimately, you need to pay strict attention to that undefinable but definite "I'm in over my head" feeling that often comes as a gut reaction. That response is nearly always accurate and should not be ignored.

5. Do you think she will be able to work in a group setting? Does she seem like she might be frightened by a strong display of emotion from another group member? Do you think she will be capable of being open with the group, once she is secure? When you first meet with her, does she completely monopolize the conversation? If you are concerned about any of these possibilities, it may be better to see her on an individual basis.

6. Was she your "pre-abortion intake"? If you are a counselor in a crisis pregnancy center setting, did you meet with this woman when she came in for a pregnancy test? Were you disappointed when she decided to abort? Do you feel awkward now about counseling her after the abortion? We would recommend that post-abortion support group leaders *not* attempt to work with women they have seen in crisis counseling because of the possibility of conflicting emotions.

7. Is she in real pain presently, or is she merely curious? It is not a requirement that a woman have crying spells twelve times a day to prove that she desperately needs to be in the group. As stated previously, many women have already worked on one or two of the task areas, but still have an intense need to resolve the pain in those remaining. Some women, depending mainly on personality, will not reveal their emotional pain in an initial interview. Others will call you and break down fifteen seconds into the conversation. An emotional display (or lack thereof) is not necessarily a valid indicator of the amount of pain being experienced.

You'll need to question carefully those women who come to you stating they want to participate in a group, but whose general presentation is somewhat "flat." If you get the definite impression that a woman wants to go through the group as part of a "self-exploration" process (and not because she is in present pain), do *not* let her participate. The other group members will feel confused and defective if she seems to be there simply out of curiosity. It might be profitable to meet with such a woman privately, however. She may have tremendous post-abortion issues but may also be adept at repressing her awareness of problems that need attention. (NOTE: It is also important not to let an "observer" participate in the group. Members must feel that *everyone* in the group, including the leader, is willing to be a full participant.)

8. Is she a teenager? It is generally preferable to work individually with a teenager, for four reasons. First, a teenager is at a developmental stage of life very different from that of an adult woman. Since she is struggling to define her own identity apart from her parents, she will tend to be far more preoccupied with herself than perhaps at any other time of her life. This self-absorption makes it difficult for her to "tune in" to others' pain.

Second, a teenager, by virtue of her young years, is probably going to be too close to her abortion experience (see next item).

Third, the abortion experience is probably the most traumatic event thus far in her young life, and the amount

94

of pain she will be experiencing may be enormous. This pain, coupled with the fact that teenagers tend to be less capable than older women of repressing maternal feelings for the fetus, can lead to a great deal of disruptive anger.

Fourth, it has been our experience that a teenager tends to feel uncomfortable in a group of adult women. An ideal situation for her would be to work in a post-abortion support group consisting entirely of teenagers. If this is not possible, you might consider meeting with her on an individual basis.

9. How long has it been since her abortion? We would highly recommend not allowing anyone who has had an abortion within the previous three months into a group, unless the group consists entirely of such women. (This time frame is given arbitrarily, and may differ from case to case). A woman who is distressed over a recent abortion is in a very different emotional state from another who has employed defense mechanisms to repress the painful emotions involved in a more distant abortion experience.

For the woman who recently aborted, the wounds are fresh, and the pain is intense and immediate. She is not going to have the patience to wait while the other group members slowly peel back the layers of repression to uncover buried emotions. It would be best to see this woman one-on-one when she makes a plea for help, allowing her to deal with the emotions immediately.

10. Is she pregnant? Since a subsequent pregnancy can be a trigger event for the onset of PAS, it is not uncommon to have at least one pregnant woman in a post-abortion support group. This should not be a problem—provided that any issues raised by her pregnancy are addressed *early* in the group's history.

A pregnant woman may feel awkward and guilty attending the meetings. Conversely, some group members may unconsciously resent the fact that she is carrying a baby while their wombs are empty. As long as the feelings on both sides can be verbalized, acknowledged, and validated, the pregnant member can participate effectively in the group setting.

11. Has she had more than one abortion? Ask her to choose the abortion that is bothering her the most at this present time (not necessarily the first one), and work on that one event by itself throughout the group. Most women who have had multiple abortions feel guilty that they are troubled by one or two of their abortions, and not so much by the other(s). Explain to her that this is quite normal, and that the degree to which each abortion plagues her depends on a number of variables—her relationship to the father of the baby, how much she wanted to keep a particular pregnancy, how coerced she felt, and the like.

Very often, as a woman deals specifically with one abortion, the forgiveness received and extended is applied to the other experiences. She will probably, however, need to grieve for each individual child. (The exception to this guideline is when a woman has experienced two or more abortions in rapid sequence—one or two months apart—and the circumstances were nearly identical in each case. In this situation, two or even three abortion experiences may in essence be "lumped together" and worked through as one episode.)

Setting Up the Group

Anyone seeking to lead a support group of any kind must be willing to learn the basic principles of group process. A little time spent reading about this subject will spare you many unpleasant mistakes.[6] We recommend *Groups: Process and Practice* by Corey and Corey, as well as the excellent book (written from a Christian worldview) *Getting Together: A Guide for Good Groups* by Em Griffin. In addition to the wisdom found in these books, we offer the following guidelines which are more specific to post-abortion support groups.

A group of four to six women seems to be ideal for this kind of intense work.[7] You should begin with four only if you feel absolutely certain that all are motivated enough to attend every session. Usually, however, most groups are made up of two or three women who appear likely to "go the distance," and another two or three who may leave early in the group experience. If you begin with four and drop down to two, you no longer have a group!

The group should remain "closed" (no new members) after the first meeting. This is necessary in order for the members to build a sense of trust with each other. If a new member is allowed to join after two or three sessions, the original participants will feel reluctant to share openly because the new member doesn't know the group's history. If someone comes to you for counseling after a group has started, either see her individually or, if possible, encourage her to wait for the next group to form.

It will take eight to twelve sessions (one and one-half hours long) to complete the *Women in Ramah* workbook, depending upon the number in the group. While you want to set definite dates for the group to put *in ink* on

[6]Perhaps the most notable book on the subject in the psychological community is Yalom's *The Theory and Practice of Group Psychotherapy*. But this is a rather formidable text for the average lay counselor.

[7]A standard textbook on group process will define the ideal size as eight to twelve people. However, it has been our experience that women suffering from PAS are so apprehensive about discussing their abortion experience they seem to be more comfortable in smaller groups.

their calendars, ask them to "pencil in" an additional session in case the group needs it. (But never have an extra session unless *all* members can attend.)

Ideally, the group should be as homogeneous as possible (e. g., all teenagers, all women who have had two or more abortions, all married women). Of course, this may not happen for a while, so you must do the best you can in the beginning, following the guidelines listed above. There are some people who definitely should NOT be in your post-abortion support group. Do not allow a husband, boyfriend, or parent to attend the sessions. They will become "lightning rods" for the group's anger when husbands, boyfriends, or parents are brought up! (It is not fair to the one boyfriend, for instance, to have several group members projecting their own "boyfriend issues" onto him.) Meet with spouses/boyfriends briefly before the group begins. Explain the process, warn them about the forthcoming mood swings, and solicit their support and understanding.

Don't conduct one-on-one counseling with any single group member while she is in the group. This sets up an unhealthy alliance between you and the one member, who will tend to share intimately only with you and not with the group. Additionally, no group member should be seeing a counselor on a one-to-one basis for the purpose of working through the abortion experience. She will tend to work the hardest during her sessions with the counselor, thus diluting the effort she is willing to put forth in the group.

We strongly recommend that you try co-leadership with another person if you are a lay counselor. The ideal combination would be a gentle but firm "confronter" and a compassionate "consoler." This works well for several reasons: one leader can pick up when the other is at a loss for direction; two counselors reviewing a group session are more likely to understand what needs to happen next; if one leader is violating any of the rules of good group management, the other can gently correct; and a spirit of teamwork keeps each individual from feeling inadequate.

Finally, a small suggestion which will make an immense difference in your group sessions: make sure your meeting room is comfortable! Is it carpeted? Have you turned off the fluorescent bulbs and added a couple of low-lit lamps? Is it private—will group members feel reluctant to cry freely for fear someone will be disturbed? These small details create an atmosphere in which the group members can feel secure and ready to share.

The First Session (Orientation)

1. **Introduce the group leader(s)—qualifications, reasons for wanting to form a post-abortion support group, etc.** If this is the first group you've led, don't be afraid to say so. (Never try to be something you are not!) Explain that a lot of information will be presented during this session, and that the real "work" will be done in the following weeks. If you have had an abortion yourself, mention this during the explanation of your reasons for wanting to help post-abortion women.

2. **Opening round.** Go around the circle and ask each member to share (briefly—no more than three minutes) how they are feeling about being here.

3. **The group's purpose.** Share how you hope the group setting will provide a safe place for each woman to remember the pain associated with her abortion decision; address the trauma, guilt, anger, and grief issues associated with that abortion; experience forgiveness; and learn new, more functional ways of dealing with the ongoing reminders of that abortion.

4. **Explain the four task areas.** Type them out and ask members to consider which task areas will require their

hardest effort. Each woman must take responsibility for the work she will do during the group's time together. You are not a magician who can pull each woman's healing out of a hat.

5. Establish rules. Type the following rules out for each person to read and affirm:

a. Confidentiality (except when a member is in danger of harming herself or others).

b. Agreement to keep up with the assigned chapters in the workbook (even though some will progress more quickly than others, for a variety of reasons).

c. Importance of consistent attendance. Explain how important it is for everyone to be there every time in order for a feeling of trust to develop within the group. If one member is absent from a session, she may feel alienated from the group to some degree. In addition, there will be an awkwardness during the next session when someone who is sharing must stop and explain what took place while the other member was gone.

d. Freedom to exit. Explain how uncomfortable it may be to come back after the first session, as some of those old, unwanted emotions begin to rise to the surface. Warn them to anticipate and fight against the temptation to quit the group. However, also make it clear that each member has the freedom to exit at any time, with the hope that she will explain to the group why she is leaving.

e. Nonjudgmental feedback. This is necessary in order to protect each member during times of vulnerability. It is your job as the leader to stop the group when harmful feedback has been given and deal with it immediately.

f. Expectation that each member will fully participate. This is coupled with the understanding that *no one* should feel coerced into sharing. Many post-abortion women have felt victimized for so long that they will avoid a setting in which they feel forced to perform for someone else.

g. No "rescuing." If a woman is remembering a long-repressed pain and is crying profusely, no one else should attempt to stop that important process by comforting her (as is the natural reaction, especially in a group of caring women). Letting her know the group is hurting with her is far more helpful than endeavoring to "make it better."

h. Don't interrupt. When one member is "on a roll" with a thought, a story, or an emotional response, another member may be tempted to "jump in" with her own new insight. The leader must carefully guard against this. It is important for the group to give feedback after someone has completely finished, but it is crucial not to allow anyone to interrupt that process. A good guideline for group feedback is first to ask the members to tell the person how they feel about what she just shared (focusing on the one who just finished). Then the members can progress to what happened to *them* while she was sharing.

6. Educate about the counseling process. The woman seeking help for PAS must understand that she is setting up an "approach/avoidance" conflict within herself by coming to the group. Part of her desperately needs to address this issue, and part of her will fight vigorously to avoid remembering the past pain. Warn the group members that their dreams (good or bad) may increase, as previously unconscious material is deliberately brought closer to the surface. Explain that they may experience periods of euphoria and/or depression as they do this work.

Ask them to secure support and understanding from their families, if possible. Also, explain to them that, in some cases, family members (particularly spouses) may not share their enthusiasm for all of the newfound understanding and insights about the abortion experience.

Finally, encourage them to increase activities which will offset possible episodes of depression. (These might include exercise, carefully planned "fun" outings with friends and family.)

7. Introduce the PACE workbooks. Ask them to complete the first two chapters prior to the next session. Those women in the group who do not have a Christian orientation will need to decide whether or not to bypass the questions which refer to Scripture. Explain that you are comfortable with whatever they choose to do, but that you believe there is a spiritual component to the healing process (even if one is not associated with a particular organized religious group). If the leader does not manifest a "hidden agenda" (i. e., "I must help this woman become a Christian"), most non-Christian group members will be comfortable using the workbook.

8. Ask each member to spend five to ten minutes telling the group a little about her abortion experience. If you have had a previous abortion, be the first to share and set the example of what you are expecting. Be very careful to enforce the time allotment, for two important reasons. First, it is crucial that *every* member have a chance to speak during the first session. Second, if a woman is permitted to share deeply for a long period of time, she may feel that she made herself vulnerable too quickly and feel reticent to return to the group.

Don't worry if someone seems to be sharing on an extremely superficial level at this point. Remember that the group members are "testing the water" for safety and acceptance, and most are not willing to drop their guard entirely on the first night. (Just admitting to a group that they've had an abortion takes a lot of courage!)

9. Closing round. Going around the circle, ask each woman for a sixty-second response to a question such as, "What did you learn about yourself tonight?" or "How are

102

you feeling right now, compared to the beginning of this session?''

Subsequent Sessions

1. **Opening round.** The PACE program provides an excellent list of suggested opening round questions. (Be creative and compose your own, if you wish.) The opening round serves two functions: it is an icebreaker which starts the group talking about feelings without getting too "heavy," and it also gives the leader(s) some information about who is most eager to work, and what the emotional "weather" is among the members as you begin a session.

2. **Discussion/sharing/feedback.** The "meat" of the sessions will consist of discussing the assigned chapter(s), sharing each person's answers to the various questions, and hearing feedback from the leader and other group members in response to the insights each member is making. While it is impossible to describe exactly how each session will progress at this point, the leader and each group member should have a clear idea of what task areas need to be covered. It should also become evident where each person is experiencing healing and where each person is getting "stuck."

Sometimes certain topics will evoke a strong emotional response in one or more group members, and the verbalization of these feelings can lead to valuable work. At other times the discussion can become rather academic (when it feels safer to talk theory than to expose one's pain). The leader's job is to keep the group focused on the work its members came to do.

3. **Homework assignment.** Assign the next one or two chapters in the workbook (depending upon the number of sessions you have decided on). If someone had difficulty completing the previous homework, urge her to work as

quickly as her emotions will allow her. There will usually be at least one group member who will not finish the workbook by the last session. No one can be pushed faster than she wants to go.

4. Closing round. The purpose of the closing round is to allow each group member to summarize her feelings about the session and the personal insights she made. Each person should be encouraged to make a final brief comment. There is a list of suggested closing rounds in the back of the workbook.

A few parting thoughts about group work are worth noting at this point. Don't be discouraged if the group members are progressing at radically different rates. This is perfectly normal. Sometimes a woman will have trouble working in one group, but will be ready to work in a later group.

The inexperienced group leader may think mistakenly that a member who has said very little during the sessions is not accomplishing anything. In most cases, a silent member is actually working very hard, "tailgating" on the work others are doing out loud and applying their insights to her own situation. Encourage quieter group members to verbalize what they have been thinking while someone else worked, but don't push if they are not ready. Send a brief note to each woman mid-week to let her know you are praying for her, and encourage her to do the assignment.

During the final session, help each woman identify the work she has done and what work remains. Spend some time talking about how each member is going to combat the ongoing memories.

Bibliography

* = recommended reading for those hurting from a past abortion

** = additional reading for those who desire to help post-abortion women

*BAKER, DON, *Beyond Choice: The Abortion Story No One Is Telling*, Portland Oregon: Multnomah Press, 1985. (This short book is a straightforward account of one woman's abortion experiences and how profoundly they continue to affect her. This book is helpful because it carefully and agonizingly documents the pain a post-abortion woman suffers; however, only a couple of pages at the very end attempt to deal with any healing she sustained.

*COCHRANE, LINDA, *Women in Ramah: A Post-Abortion Bible Study*. Falls Church, Virginia: Christian Action Council Education and Ministries Fund, 1987. (This is the best workbook that we've come across so far for use in groups. The chapters cover all the task areas mentioned in this volume.)

**COLLINS, GARY R., *Can You Trust Psychology?* Downers Grove, Illinois: InterVarsity Press, 1988. (The author has done an admirable job delineating the growing hostility in some quarters between theology and psychology, and he defuses the debate by demonstrating how the two areas are completely compatible. Required reading for any lay counselor operating in an environment where the word "psychology" is anathema.)

*ERVIN, PAULA, *Women Exploited: The Other Victims of Abortion*. Huntington, Indiana: Our Sunday Visitor, Inc., 1985. (A poignant collection of case histories from women who have come through

WEBA groups. Lists WEBA and Right To Life chapters around the country.)

**GRIFFIN, EM, *Getting Together: A Guide for Good Groups*. Downers Grove, Illinois: InterVarsity Press, 1982. (Our best recommendation for learning about group process. Written from a Christian perspective, this book is easily understood and is a valuable tool for the lay counselor endeavoring to lead a group.)

KOERBEL, PAM, *Abortion's Second Victim*. Wheaton, Illinois: Victor Books, 1986. (This volume includes the author's personal account of her abortion experience and subsequent healing, a helpful section on what motivates women to abort, and a moving explanation of how to accept God's forgiveness.)

**MALL, DAVID, and WALTER F. WATTS, *The Psychological Aspects of Abortion*. Washington, D.C.: University Publications of America, 1979. (Although dated at this point, this book retains an important place on the bookshelf of those who want to know about the earlier studies investigating the existence of PAS.)

*MANNION, MICHAEL T., *Abortions and Healing: A Cry To Be Whole*. Kansas City, Missouri: Sheed and Ward, 1986. (Another excellent resource for the woman who hurts from a past abortion. Father Mannion has been a pioneer in this field.)

*McCLUNG, FLOYD, JR., *The Father Heart of God*. Eugene, Oregon: Harvest House Publishers, 1985. (The importance of this book cannot be overestimated, especially for one working with women who have a Christian worldview. This elegantly written volume does a magnificent job of correcting the reader's misperceptions of a judgmental God and replacing it with an approachable image of God as a loving father.)

*MICHELS, NANCY, *Helping Women Recover from Abortion*. Minneapolis, Minnesota: Bethany House Publishers, 1988. (This excellent book includes, among other topics, a commendable explanation of the grieving process through which the post-abortion woman proceeds. It also contains a much needed chapter on how abortion affects others involved in the abortion decision.)

**MINIRTH, FRANK B., and PAUL D. MEIER, *Happiness Is a Choice*. Grand Rapids, Michigan: Baker Book House, 1978. (This manual describing the symptoms, causes, and cures of depression is the best of its kind, in our opinion. Drs. Minirth and Meier have written in a style easily understood by anyone. This is a basic tool for any counselor dealing with depressed clients.)

**NOUWEN, HENRI J. M., *The Wounded Healer*. Garden City, New York: Image Books, 1979. (Although not specifically written on the subject of post-abortion trauma, this tiny book is required reading for anyone attempting to deal with the emotional suffering of another human being. We cannot praise this little monograph highly enough as a basic primer for all would-be counselors!)

*PERETTI, FRANK E., *Tilly*. Westchester, Illinois: Crossway Books, 1988. (This short novel describes "Kathy's" dream/vision as she meets the child she aborted years ago. While scripturally unsound in depicting the child saddened while a resident in heaven, it is both touching and powerful in its depiction of the process of grieving for an aborted baby. The story concludes on a note of great hope.)

**REARDON, DAVID, *Aborted Women: Silent No More*. Chicago, Illinois: Loyola University Press, 1987. (Dr. Reardon discusses the results of a survey administered to post-abortion women through WEBA chapters in many different states. In addition, there are several well-written chapters with such provocative titles as "Feminists Who Abort," "The Impact of Abortion on Later Children," and "Before and After Legalization." Excellent case studies are included to illustrate his points.)

**SALTENBERGER, ANN, *Every Woman Has a Right to Know the Dangers of Legal Abortion*. Glassboro, New Jersey: Air-Plus Enterprises, 1983. (Written to the woman contemplating an abortion, Ms. Saltenberger minces no words as she lists the documented complications of early and late abortions. The book stresses a woman's right to full disclosure. Although documentation isn't current, this book is still an eye-opener and for many years was almost the only book of its kind on the market.)

**SCANLAN, MICHAEL, *Inner Healing*. New York: Paulist Press, 1974. (Particularly helpful in dealing with the woman who has a strong, intact Christian worldview. While not mentioning abortion specifically, the book addresses the issue of acute spiritual pain and how the Christian counselor can deal with that pain.)

**SHOSTAK, ARTHUR, and GARY McCLOUTH, *Men and Abortion*. New York: Praeger Publishers, 1984. (Dr. Shostak surveyed 1,000 men as they waited for their partners to get abortions. In addition, 75 post-abortion men were interviewed about the aftermath of their abortion experiences. This book rocked the pro-life camp because Dr. Shostak, a strong pro-choice advocate, reported that a strong majority of the men he surveyed were having problems with the abortion. However, the book operates wholly on the premise that if men—and, presumably, women—were only given better pre-abortion counseling, most of these problems could be eliminated. A valuable tool for those hoping to work with post-abortion victims; just be aware of the strong pro-choice ideology.)

**SPECKHARD, ANNE, *Psycho-Social Stress Following Abortion*. Kansas City, Missouri: Sheed and Ward, 1987. (Dr. Speckhard's significant study of how abortion affects behavior is described and summarized.)

*STANFORD, SUSAN M., *Will I Cry Tomorrow?* Old Tappan, New Jersey: Fleming Revell Co., 1986. (The author's own experience with an abortion and subsequent post-abortion trauma. Beautifully written from a Catholic viewpoint, Dr. Stanford elegantly describes the inner healing she finally experienced and outlines healing steps for the reader.)

Where to Find Help

* = **information on PAS**

** = **information and Counseling for PAS**

ABORTION TRAUMA SERVICES AND OUTREACH**
1608 13th Ave. S. #112
Birmingham, Alabama 35202
(205) 939-0302
(Associated with Sav-A-Life)

AMERICAN VICTIMS OF ABORTION[1]
Olivia Gans, Director
419 7th St., NW Suite 402
Washington, DC 20004
(202) 626-8800

ASSOCIATION FOR INTERDISCIPLINARY RESEARCH IN VALUES AND SOCIAL CHANGE*[2]
Wanda Franz, Ph.D., President
419 7th Street NW #500
Washington, DC 20004
(202) 626-8800

---

[1] Excellent national organization geared toward public awareness of PAS. The organization is attempting to create a networking of PAS counselors on a national level. Also request "Olivia's Story."

[2] An organization made up of pro-life professionals and researchers. Newsletter is great.

CHRISTIAN ACTION COUNCIL[3]
701 W. Broad St., #405
Falls Church, Virginia 22046
(703) 237-2100

LEN CROOK
The Women's Recovery Center
15900 Grand Ave.
Lake Elsinore, CA 92330
(714) 678-3688

HEALING VISIONS NETWORK*[4]
National Youth Pro-Life Coalition
Jackson Avenue
Hastings on Hudson, NY 10706
(914) 478-0103

HUMAN LIFE INTERNATIONAL*[5]
7845-E Airpark Rd.
Gaithersburg, MD 20879
(301) 670-7884

OPEN ARMS (Abortion-Related Ministries)**
National Headquarters
6919 E. 10th St. F-10
Indianapolis, IN 46219
(317) 359-9950

DAVE AND CATHY PISANIC**
Center for Creative Christian Living
1917 Reistertown Rd.
Owings Mills, MD 21117
(301) 363-6960

[3]Source for the post-abortion Bible study, *Women in Ramah* and
information on how to start a PACE—Post Abortion Counseling and
Education—program.
[4]Source of excellent tapes from their annual Healing Visions
Conferences.
[5]HLI produces a quarterly newsletter focusing on post-abortion
issues.

PROJECT RACHAEL**
c/o Respect Life Office
Archdiocese of Milwaukee
P.O. Box 2018
Milwaukee, WI 53201
(414) 769-3391

LINDA ROSS**
Renewal Counseling
625 N. Second Ave.
Tucson, AZ 85705
(602) 791-9971

DR. VINCENT RUE**[6]
Sir Thomas More Marriage and Family Clinic
Downey Professional Building
10603 Downey Ave. #200
Downey, CA 90241
(213) 923-0341

TERRY SELBY, M.S.W.**[7]
Counseling Associates of Bemidji
P.O. Box 577
Bemidji, MN 56601
(218) 751-9510

DR. ANNE SPECKHARD**
Family Systems Center
5053 S. 12th Street
Arlington, VA 22204
phone number??

SR. PAULA VANDEGAER
Living World Publications Office
2606 1/2 West 8th Street
Los Angeles, CA 90057
(213) 382-2156

---

[6]Dr. Rue is widely recognized and respected for his work with PAS. He has written numerous excellent articles and brochures, particularly concerning the effects of abortion on men and other family members.

[7]An in-patient setting for treatment of PAS.

VICTIMS OF CHOICE**
Nola Jones, Director
124 Shefield Dr.
Vacaville, CA 95688
(707) 448-6015

WEBA (Women Exploited by Abortion)
24823 Nogal St.
Morena Valley, CA 92388
(714) 247-1278

IN CANADA:
ABORTION OUTREACH CENTRE
524 Queen Alexandra Way SE
Calgary, Alberta T2J 4C8

IN THE UNITED KINGDOM:
BRITISH VICTIMS OF ABORTION
S.P.U.C.
7 Tufton Street
London, SW1P 3QN England